T0334271

Non-Governmental Organisations and the United Nations Human Rights System

Non-governmental organisations (NGOs) have become important, if sometimes overlooked, actors in international human rights law. Although NGOs are not generally provided for in the hard law of treaties, they use the UN human rights system to hold Governments to account. A key way in which they do so is using State-reporting mechanisms, initially the UN treaty bodies, but more recently supplemented by the Human Rights Council's Universal Periodic Review. In doing so, NGOs provide information and contribute to developing recommendations. NGOs also lobby for new treaties, contribute to the drafting of these treaties, and bring individual complaints to the UN human rights bodies.

This book charts the historical development of the NGO role in the UN. It examines the UN regulation of NGOs but largely the informal nature of the role, and an exploration of the various types of NGOs, including some less benign actors, such as GONGOs (Governmental NGOs). It also draws on empirical data to illustrate NGO influence on UN human rights bodies and gives voice to stakeholders both inside and outside the UN. The book concludes that the current UN human rights system is heavily reliant on NGOs and that they play an essential fact-finding role and contribute to global democratisation and governance.

Dr. Fiona McGaughey is Senior Lecturer at the University of Western Australia Law School.

Routledge Research in Human Rights Law

For more information about this series, please visit: www.routledge.com/ Routledge-Research-in-Human-Rights-Law/book-series/HUMRIGHTSLAW

Non-Governmental Organisations and the United Nations Human Rights System

Fiona McGaughey

Routledge
Taylor & Francis Group

LONDON AND NEW YORK

First published 2021
by Routledge
2 Park Square, Milton Park, Abingdon, Oxon OX14 4RN

and by Routledge
605 Third Avenue, New York, NY 10158

Routledge is an imprint of the Taylor & Francis Group, an informa business

© 2021 Fiona McGaughey .

British Library Cataloguing-in-Publication Data
A catalogue record for this book is available from the British Library

Library of Congress Cataloging-in-Publication Data
A catalog record for this book has been requested

ISBN: 978-1-138-36009-9 (hbk)
ISBN: 978-1-032-01220-9 (pbk)
ISBN: 978-0-429-43332-0 (ebk)

Typeset in Galliard
by Apex CoVantage, LLC

Contents

Acknowledgements

This book is the result of several years of research and my previous experience of working in the NGO sector. I am indebted to the many people over this period who supported me, provided feedback on my research, or shared their networks, in particular Adjunct Professor Holly Cullen, Ms Anastasia Crickley, Professor Stephen Smith, Associate Professor Amy Maguire, Dr Emma Larking, Mr Morten Kjaerum, and Assistant Professor Philipp Kastner. I was grateful to receive the Leah Jane Cohen Bursary from Graduate Women (Western Australia) which helped fund travel to Geneva for my research and would like to thank all those who supported my field work and participated in interviews. Finally, a special thanks for all their support to my mum and dad and to Conleth, Cahir, Daire, and Máidhe O'Loughlin.

1   Introduction

1 Introduction

There has been a growing interest in non-state actors in international law,[1] and in international human rights law, it has become clear that non-governmental organisations (NGOs) play a significant role.[2] In a largely voluntary system, bereft of enforcement mechanisms, NGOs hold Governments to account on their human rights obligations – monitoring 'from below', often using mechanisms of the United Nations ('UN') which monitors 'from above'. Yet, despite the critical role played by NGOs, in the past it has often been overlooked in traditional doctrinal scholarship. That it is overlooked by lawyers is perhaps not surprising as with the exception of the limited opportunities provided for 'consultation' with NGOs in Article 71 of the UN Charter,[3] there are almost no hard law provisions for the NGO role in subsequent human rights treaties. A theme in doctrinal scholarship on NGOs has been on the question of whether they have international legal personality and there is a lack of consensus on the answer to this question.[4] This book is more concerned with fully understanding the nature

---

1 See, e.g. Math Noortmann, August Reinisch and Cedric Ryngaert (eds), *Non-State Actors in International Law* (Hart Publishing, 2015).

2 David P Forsythe, *Human Rights in International Relations* (Cambridge University Press, 2006) 203–4; Michael Freeman, *Human Rights: An Interdisciplinary Approach* (Polity Press, 2011) 152; Laurie S Wiseberg, 'The Role of Non-Governmental Organizations (NGOs) in the Protection and Enforcement of Human Rights' in Janusz Symonides (ed), *Human Rights: International Protection, Monitoring, Enforcement* (UNESCO Publishing, 2003) 347, 350 ('Role of NGOs in Protection of Human Rights').

3 *Charter of the United Nations.*

4 See, e.g. Christine Bakker and Luisa Vierucci, 'Introduction: A Normative or Pragmatic Definition of NGOs?' in Pierre-Marie Dupuy and Luisa Vierucci (eds), *NGOs in International Law: Efficiency in Flexibility* (Edward Elgar Publishing, 2008) 1 ('*NGOs in International Law*').

of the NGO *role* and *influence* in international human rights law and, in particular, the UN human rights system.

NGOs began as almost extraneous to this system but have carved out a role for themselves in the international human rights framework, welcomed by the UN,[5] but often resisted by States.[6] In the last 70 years, they have become increasingly important. In 1994, the UN Secretary General noted that 'NGO involvement has not only justified the inclusion of Article 71 [of the UN Charter] . . . but that it has far exceeded the original scope of these legal provisions'.[7] NGOs have been influential in drafting international legislation,[8] in bringing individual complaints to treaty bodies,[9] and in the State-reporting processes of the UN human rights treaty bodies and the Human Rights Council's Universal Periodic Review.[10] The UN human rights treaties as a primary source of international human rights law are germane to the analysis of the human rights work of NGOs. There are nine core human rights treaties at the time of writing, with discussions underway on at least a further two.[11]

5 *Strengthening of the United Nations System*, 58th sess, Agenda Item 59, UN Doc A/58/817 (11 June 2004).

6 Eduard Jordaan, 'South Africa and the United Nations Human Rights Council' (2014) 36(1) *Human Rights Quarterly* 90.

7 *General Review of Arrangements for Consultations with Non-Governmental Organisations: Report of the Secretary General*, 1st sess, Agenda Item 3, UN Doc E/AC.70/1994/5 (26 May 1994).

8 Cynthia Price Cohen, 'The Role of Nongovernmental Organizations in the Drafting of the Convention on the Rights of the Child' (1990) 12(1) *Human Rights Quarterly* 137–47; Zoe N Pearson, *Global Civil Society and International Law-Making: Mapping the Boundaries* (PhD Thesis, Australian National University, 2002).

9 Hurst Hannum (ed), *Guide to International Human Rights Practice* (University of Philadelphia Press, 1984); Loveday Hodson, *NGOs and the Struggle for Human Rights in Europe* (Hart Publishing, 2011).

10 Fiona McGaughey, 'Advancing, Retreating or Stepping on Each Other's Toes? The Role of Non-Governmental Organisations in United Nations Human Rights Treaty Body Reporting and the Universal Periodic Review' (2017) 35 *Australian Yearbook of International Law* 187; Fiona McGaughey, 'The Role and Influence of Non-Governmental Organisations in the Universal Periodic Review – International Context and Australian Case Study' (2017) 17(3) *Human Rights Law Review* 421.

11 The nine core treaties are, ordered by date of adoption by the General Assembly: *International Convention on the Elimination of All Forms of Racial Discrimination*, opened for signature 21 December 1965, 660 UNTS 195 (entered into force 4 January 1969) ('ICERD'); *International Covenant on Civil and Political Rights*, opened for signature 16 December 1966, 999 UNTS 171 (entered into force 23 March 1976) ('ICCPR'); *International Covenant on Economic, Social and Cultural Rights*, opened for signature 16 December 1966, 993 UNTS 3 (entered into force 3 January 1976) ('ICESCR'); *Convention on the Elimination of All Forms of Discrimination against Women*, opened for signature 1 March 1980, 1249 UNTS 13 (entered into force 3 September 1981) ('CEDAW');

Despite this influential NGO role, international law has traditionally been understood as the law primarily governing relations among States. Similarly, States have traditionally been viewed as the primary, if not only, actors in, and subjects of, international law.[12] A key limitation of the State-centrism of international law is in understanding the role of non-State actors, including NGOs.[13] State-centric theories of international law remain influential but are subject to challenges. Slaughter, for example, reimagines State sovereignty as a disaggregated sovereignty and argues that the concept of the unitary State is a useful myth.[14]

In practice, it is clear that NGOs play an expansive role in contemporary society, at grassroots level, globally, and in between. They are significant actors in international development,[15] in peacebuilding,[16] in providing supports and services at a local level,[17] and in 'naming and shaming' governments and businesses who breach human rights.[18] They are also instrumental

---

International Convention against Torture and Other Cruel, Inhuman and Degrading Treatment or Punishment, opened for signature 10 December 1984, 1465 UNTS 85 (entered into force 26 June 1987) ('CAT'); *Convention on the Rights of the Child,* opened for signature 20 November 1989, 1577 UNTS 3 (entered into force 2 September 1990) ('CRoC'); *International Convention on the Protection of the Rights of All Migrant Workers and Members of their Families,* opened for signature 18 December 1990, 2220 UNTS 3 (entered into force 1 July 2003); *International Convention for the Protection of All Persons from Enforced Disappearance,* opened for signature 20 December 2006, 2716 UNTS 3 (entered into force 23 December 2010); *Convention on the Rights of Persons with Disabilities,* opened for signature 13 December 2006, 2515 UNTS 3 (entered into force 3 May 2008).

12 See, e.g. Malcolm N Shaw, *International Law* (Cambridge University Press, 2008) 1; Donald R Rothwell et al, *International Law: Cases and Materials with Australian Perspectives* (Cambridge University Press, 2nd ed, 2014) 1.

13 Pearson (n 8) 87.

14 Anne-Marie Slaughter, *A New World Order* (Princeton University Press, 2004).

15 Harmut Elsenhans and Hannes Warnecke-Berger, 'Non-Governmental Development Organisations' in Aynsley Kellow and Hannah Murphy-Gregory (eds), *Handbook of Research on NGOs* (Edward Elgar Publishing, 2018) 150.

16 See, e.g. Thania Paffenholz (ed), *Civil Society & Peacebuilding: A Critical Assessment* (Lynne Rienner Publishers, 2010); Renee Jeffery, Lia Kent and Joanne Wallis, 'Reconceiving the Roles of Religious Civil Society Organizations in Transitional Justice: Evidence from the Solomon Islands, Timor-Leste and Bougainville' (2017) 11(3) *International Journal of Transitional Justice* 378.

17 See, e.g. Susan Goodwin and Ruth Phillips, 'The Marketisation of Human Services and the Expansion of the Not-For-Profit Sector' in Gabrielle Meagher and Susan Goodwin (eds), *Markets, Rights and Power in Australian Social Policy* (Sydney University Press, 2015).

18 See, e.g. James Meernik et al, 'The Impact of Human Rights Organizations on Naming and Shaming Campaigns' (2012) 56(2) *Journal of Conflict Resolution* 233; Cullen Hendrix and Wendy Wong, 'When Is the Pen Truly Mighty? Regime Type and the Efficacy of Naming and Shaming in Curbing Human Rights Abuses' (2013) 43(3) *British Journal of Political Science* 651.

in mobilising the public to take action regarding human rights abuses,[19] in carrying out research on human rights issues,[20] in influencing policy development,[21] in lobbying for people's rights, in taking cases on behalf of those whose rights have been breached, and in acting as *amicus curiae* for courts.[22] The list goes on. And in many of these roles, they contribute to realising people's human rights – including civil and political rights, and economic, social, and cultural rights. As such, NGOs can rightly be understood as significant for human rights promotion and protection, even if some NGOs do not specifically identify as 'human rights NGOs', or even resist concepts of rights. The specific focus of this book is the NGO engagement with key international human rights bodies at the UN in order to better understand the NGO role and influence.

This chapter briefly outlines the methodology used for the book, introduces the reader to types and definitions of NGOs, and scopes the existing literature on NGOs, before outlining the structure for the remainder of the book.

2 Methodology

This book is a sociolegal study of the role and influence of NGOs in the UN human rights system. Research for the book draws on some elements of my PhD thesis (2014–2017), extended to cover broader themes and further analysis (2018–2020). The methods used include doctrinal analysis of international legal instruments and materials and empirical legal research involving field trips to Geneva for observation of UN fora and interviews with key stakeholders.[23] Semi-structured interviews carried out with key stakeholders were central to the qualitative data gathering for the book and

---

19 See, e.g. the work of Amnesty International at *Amnesty International* <www.amnesty. org/en/>.

20 See, e.g. the reports published by international NGO Human Rights Watch at *Human Rights Watch* <www.hrw.org/publications>.

21 See, e.g. Cecilia Tortajada, 'Nongovernmental Organizations and Influence on Global Public Policy' (2016) 3(2) *Asia and the Pacific Policy Studies* 266.

22 See, e.g. Nicole Bürli, *Third-Party Interventions before the European Court of Human Rights: Amicus Curiae, Member-State and Third-Party Interventions* (Intersentia, 2017).

23 For discussion of doctrinal and sociolegal methods, see, e.g. Terry Hutchinson and Nigel Duncan, 'Defining and Describing What We Do: Doctrinal Legal Research' (2012) 17(1) *Deakin Law Review* 83; Christopher McCrudden, 'Legal Research and the Social Sciences' (2006) 122 *Law Quarterly Review* 632; Anne Orford, 'On International Legal Method' (2013) 1 *London Review of International Law* 166; Peter Cane and Herbert M Kritzer (eds), *The Oxford Handbook of Empirical Legal Research* (Oxford University Press, 2010) 1.

particularly informed Chapter 4 on treaties and treaty bodies, and Chapter 5 on the UN Human Rights Council. Twenty-six semi-structured interviews were carried out in 2015 and 2016 with stakeholders relevant to the NGO role in UN human rights bodies, including staff in the UN Office of the High Commissioner for Human Rights (OHCHR), State representatives, treaty body independent experts, NGOs, and a National Human Rights Institution (NHRI). Interviewees were primarily selected using purposeful sampling, due to their direct participation in, or experience working with, the selected UN bodies, and through snowball sampling when interviewees nominated other potential interviewees.[24] Unlike quantitative research, qualitative research of this nature is concerned with developing rich understanding through interviews, rather than with having a representative sample.[25] The use of mixed methods allowed for methodological triangulation – using various methods of data collection as a check on the quality or veracity of data, assuming that any weaknesses in one set of data will be addressed by the others.[26]

The research received university ethics approval and as part of this, interviewees were given the option to remain anonymous, which many did.[27] Interview data was transcribed, coded, and thematically analysed using *NVivo* qualitative analysis software.[28] In some chapters of this book, I have included not only summary themes and analysis from the interviews, but also the voice to the interviewees by relying quite heavily on quotations at times. Gillham refers to this as 'letting the interviewees speak for themselves'.[29]

Some chapters draw on my previous empirical analyses that tracked NGO influence in terms of written reports to UN treaty bodies and the Human Rights Council, identifying where NGO reports were used as the source of recommendations by the UN body. There is a well-established difficulty in determining the impact or influence of activities described broadly as

24 Uwe Flick, *Designing Qualitative Research* (Sage Publications, 2007) 27; David L Morgan, 'Snowball Sampling' in Lisa M Given (ed), *The Sage Encyclopedia of Qualitative Research Methods* (Sage, 2008)816, 816–7.

25 Zina O'Leary, *The Essential Guide to Doing your Research Project* (Sage, 2nd ed, 2014) 186; Lisa Webley, 'Qualitative Approaches to Empirical Legal Research' in Cane and Kritzer (eds) (n 23) 926.

26 Paulette M Rothbauer, 'Triangulation' in Lisa M Given (ed), *The Sage Encyclopedia of Qualitative Research Methods* (Sage Publications, 2008) 892.

27 Human Research Ethics Approval (RA/4/1/7183) University of Western Australia (November 2014).

28 See, e.g. Alan Bryman, *Social Research Methods* (Oxford University Press, 3rd ed, 2008) Ch 25 'Computer Assisted Qualitative Analysis: Using NVivo' 598.

29 Bill Gillham, *Research Interview* (Continuum International Publishing Group, 2000) 74.

'advocacy'.[30] Some writers rely on hypothesising on the counterfactual: if human rights NGOs had *not* existed, human rights would presumably have a less salient position internationally.[31] Although some authors conclude that there is no way to accurately measure human rights impact in any multi-causal situation,[32] the pragmatic approach taken by other scholars in analyses of the influence of civil society organisations (CSOs) on the UPR is useful:

> it is not possible to prove causation, i.e. whether states made these recommendations as a result of the CSO suggested recommendations. However, examination of the extent to which CSO concerns are reflected in state recommendations can at least demonstrate the level to which CSO interests are correlated and thus represented, in the process.[33]

3 Defining and categorising NGOs[34]

From the list of NGO activities earlier, we can see that NGOs are heterogeneous. Overall, a challenge of discussing the NGO role is that despite NGO being a commonly used term, there is a lack of consensus on its definition. Further, the NGO concept itself is primarily a Western one in origin and may be foreign to many Indigenous communities and in many developing countries.[35] Article 71 of the UN Charter is credited as introducing the term 'NGO' but did not provide a definition. Also, the varied nature of NGOs and the broad scope of work they undertake do not support a generic definition.

---

30 Steven Teles and Mark Schmitt, 'The Elusive Craft of Evaluating Advocacy' (2011) 9(3) *Stanford Social Innovation Review* 38. See also Forsythe (n 2) 200.

31 Forsythe (n 2) 204.

32 Laurie S Wiseberg and Harry M Scoble, 'Recent Trends in the Expanding Universe of NGOs Dedicated to the Protection of Human Rights' in Ved P Nanda, James R Scarritt and George W Shepherd Jr (eds), *Global Human Rights: Public Policies, Comparative Measures, and NGO Strategies* (Routledge, 1981) 257.

33 McMahon et al, *The Universal Periodic Review: Do Civil Society Organization-Suggested Recommendations Matter?* (Dialogue on Globalization, Friedrich-Ebert-Stiftung, November 2013) 5.

34 Some of this section is adapted and summarised from: Fiona McGaughey, 'From Gatekeepers to GONGOs: A Taxonomy of Non-Governmental Organisations Engaging with United Nations Human Rights Mechanisms' (2018) 36(2) *Netherlands Quarterly of Human Rights* 111.

35 Antonio Donini, 'The Bureaucracy and the Free Spirits: Stagnation and Innovation in the Relationship between the UN and NGOs' (1995) 16(3) *Third World Quarterly* 421, 430.

Some early scholarship on NGOs grappled with the definition and ontology of NGOs. Some understood NGOs as a balance to the power of the State, describing them as 'organizations that operate as an essential break on the juggernaut of state power',[36] or that 'act as a solvent against the strictures of sovereignty'.[37] Meanwhile, applied definitions in the form of criteria for accreditation for NGO consultative status were being developed by the UN through the Economic and Social Council ('ECOSOC').[38] ECOSOC Resolution 1996/31 did offer the following definition:

> Any such organization that is not established by a governmental entity or intergovernmental agreement shall be considered a non-governmental organization for the purpose of these arrangements, including organizations that accept members designated by governmental authorities, provided that such membership does not interfere with the free expression of the views of the organization.[39]

As discussed further in Chapter 3, ECOSOC Resolution 1996/31 also introduced conditions for NGOs to gain ECOSOC accreditation, including the requirement that the NGO's aims be in conformity with the UN Charter, that it has a democratically adopted constitution and representative structure and recognised standing in a particular field.[40]

Despite this, it is acknowledged that a range of definitions of NGOs in international law exist,[41] and that there is a lack of consensus among scholars. Such is the complexity of defining NGOs that in 2002, Kersten Martens questioned whether it was in fact 'mission impossible'.[42] This lack of definitional clarity can have knock-on effects for the potential regulation of the NGO role in the UN human rights system, again discussed further

---

36 Laurie S Wiseberg, 'Protecting Human Rights Activists and NGOs: What More Can Be Done?' (1991) 13(4) *Human Rights Quarterly* 525.

37 Steve Charnovitz, 'Nongovernmental Organizations and International Law' (2006) 100(2) *American Journal of International Law* 348, 348.

38 *Consultative Relationship between the United Nations and Non-Governmental Organizations,* ESC Res 1996/31, 49th plen mtg, UN Doc E/RES/1996/31 (25 July 1996).

39 Ibid para 12.

40 Ibid paras 2, 9–12.

41 See, e.g. Daniel Thuerer, 'The Emergence of Non-Governmental Organizations and Transnational Enterprises in International Law and the Changing Role of the State' in Rainer Hoffman (ed), *Non-State Actors as New Subjects of International Law* (Duncker & Humblot, 1999) 53; Anna-Karin Lindblom, *Non-Governmental Organisations in International Law* (Cambridge University Press, 2005), ch 1.3.

42 Kerstin Martens, 'Mission Impossible? Defining Non-Governmental Organizations' (2002) 13(3) *Voluntas: International Journal of Voluntary and Nonprofit Organizations* 271.

in Chapter 3. With regard to the broad field of international law, Dupuy and Vierucci advocate for maintaining flexibility in both the legal status and definition of NGOs for their relationships with international legal institutions, but introducing some degree of regulation for their participation before international (quasi-)judicial bodies.[43]

Although the UN now more commonly uses the broader umbrella term 'civil society',[44] this term can refer to a range of actors, including National Human Rights Institutions. For clarity, this book focuses on NGOs rather than civil society more broadly. In particular, it is interested in NGO engagement with, and influence on, UN human rights mechanisms.

As a starting point for understanding the NGO role at the UN, I developed a taxonomy of NGOs; see Diagram 1. This was specifically based on analysis of NGOs in the Human Rights Council and treaty body State-reporting systems. Sometimes NGOs fit into more than one category, and/or perform functions that can be identified with more than one category. Although the words 'domestic' and 'international' are used in the taxonomy, these could sometimes be interchanged with the word 'regional'.

(a) International facilitative

International facilitative NGOs play a useful role, both for UN bodies and for domestic NGOs. These NGOs often have a presence in Geneva where the HRC and treaty bodies sit in session. They use their expertise, knowledge of the system, and networks to facilitate engagement between domestic NGOs and the UN bodies. They may provide training to domestic NGOs, arrange interpreting and set up meetings with Committee members in the case of treaty bodies, or government representatives in the case of the UPR. Sometimes they can provide resources, such as report drafting or editing, and financial support and resources to domestic NGOs. They are mostly used by domestic dependent NGOs (e), although some domestic self-sufficient NGOs (d) are aware of the benefits of collaborating with international facilitative NGOs.

---

43 Pierre-Marie Dupuy and Luisa Vierucci, 'Introduction: A Normative or Pragmatic Definition of NGOs?' in *NGOs in International Law* (n 4) 1, 17.

44 Civil society includes, *inter alia*, NGOs, human rights defenders, victim groups, faith-based groups, unions, and research institutes such as universities. See Office of the High Commissioner for Human Rights, *Working with the United Nations Human Rights Programme: A Handbook for Civil Society* (United Nations, 2008) vii <www.ohchr.org/EN/AboutUs/CivilSociety/Documents/Handbook_en.pdf>.

In some cases, international facilitative NGOs will speak on behalf of a domestic NGO without disclosing their identity, where speaking out would put that NGO at risk of reprisals.

However, what is clear is that international facilitative NGOs do not speak on behalf of domestic NGOs without their consent, nor do they manage, control, or restrict the engagement of domestic NGOs. This is what differentiates them from either gatekeeper (b) or imperialist (c) NGOs.

The ethos and *modus operandi* of international facilitative NGOs emerge as the preferred options for most interviewees, particularly those at the UN receiving NGO information and engaging with NGOs. Some OHCHR staff and treaty body members expressed a preference for domestic NGO input being channelled through an international NGO as they felt this brought added legitimacy and credibility.

(b) Gatekeepers

Gatekeeper NGOs can at times play a role similar to the international facilitative NGOs (a) but differ in that they exercise more control over other NGOs within UN human rights State-reporting mechanisms. In particular, they can act as a gatekeeper by being prescriptive about access to UN human rights bodies or related meetings, by controlling access and potentially preventing access to them.

Gatekeepers, whether NGOs or part of the UN system, arise out of a perceived need. As noted earlier, there has been an exponential growth in the number of NGOs over the past 70 years, many of them seeking to engage with the UN system, and there is a practical need to manage this engagement. It can also be argued that gatekeeping arises due to the lack of regulation of the NGO sector. This is discussed further in Chapter 3.

(c) Imperialist

A number of interviewees expressed concern about what the author terms imperialist NGOs in the taxonomy. These are the international NGOs who present information on the human rights situation within a given State, often without domestic NGO permission or adequate consultation with them. They are often Western NGOs and do not necessarily have a presence in the State under review. The risk of international legal imperialism in international civil society has previously been identified[45] and is a critique of

---

45   Kenneth Anderson and David Rieff, ' "Global Civil Society": A Sceptical View' in Helmut Anheier et al (eds), *Global Civil Society* (Sage Publications, 2004) 26.

many popular civil society movements, including feminism which has been described as steeped in the story of imperialism and its racial assumptions.[46] The concept of imperialist NGOs is more acknowledged in the international development sector than in the human rights sector[47]: 'Donors have gained the power to set the development agenda and NGOs have slowly become Trojan horses for global neo-liberalism.'[48]

In some cases, international facilitative (a) and imperialist NGOs (c) can play a similar role. For example, international NGOs may be required in some areas of the UN where they have more access due to having ECOSOC general consultative status. Also, where there is weak civil society in a State, both international NGOs fill that gap by submitting a report based on their research.

As discussed later in this chapter, initially there was a strong focus on international NGOs in the UN system and there were fewer domestic NGOs with the capacity to engage with the UN system. However, this is less often the case now.

(d) Domestic self-sufficient

Many interviewees, including government representatives and international NGOs, attested to the expertise of some domestic NGOs. These NGOs are both experts in the domestic human rights issues and experienced in using the UN human rights bodies. They actively engage with UN human rights State-reporting mechanisms. They generally have (or can source) the funds to travel to Geneva and recognise the benefits of using international networks, such as international facilitative NGOs, although they are not reliant on them. Domestic self-sufficient NGOs may lead or play an active role in domestic NGO coalitions. Although they could submit their own reports, they recognise the benefits of working in coalitions – such as the UN's preference for coalition reports, the added legitimacy it brings, and the longer-term benefits of developing networks and partnerships for advocacy work.

Even where domestic NGOs are self-sufficient, they may have to co-operate with gatekeeper NGOs (b) or may have their views heard more effectively by liaising with an international facilitative NGO (a).

---

46 Antoinette Burton, *Race, Empire, and the Making of Western Feminism* (Routledge, 2016).

47 For a harsh critique, see James Petras, 'NGOs: In the Service of Imperialism' (1999) 29(4) *Journal of Contemporary Asia* 429.

48 Glen W Wright, 'NGOs and Western Hegemony: Causes for Concern and Ideas for Change' (2012) 22(1) *Development in Practice* 123.

(e) Domestic dependent

Interviewees spoke about domestic dependent NGOs – those who require other NGOs to assist them in engaging with the system. They can work with domestic self sufficient NGOs (d) and/or with international facilitative NGOs (a) in coalitions, or they can use international facilitative NGOs (a) to engage directly with the UN. The international facilitative NGOs interviewed identified that domestic dependent NGOs often require training and assistance to engage with UN bodies. For example, the groups experiencing discrimination and human rights abuses may have a number of access barriers, including literacy, language and resourcing. International facilitative NGOs will also sometimes help draft or edit the domestic dependent NGO's reports to UN human rights bodies.

Where this assistance has not been available or availed of, and domestic dependent NGOs have submitted reports directly to the UN body, this can be a source of frustration. This was commented on by OHCHR staff and treaty body members interviewed. One interviewee gave an example of receiving three NGO reports 'each quite long and not very good, sometimes confusing'.[49] In these cases, in the absence of any supports from the UN bodies due to their lack of funding, engaging with domestic self-sufficient NGOs (d) and international facilitative NGOs (a) can be mutually beneficial. With increasing technology and access to information and networks, the number of domestic dependent NGOs can be expected to decrease, or they could quite rapidly become domestic self-sufficient (d).

(f) Governmental non-governmental organisations (GONGOs)

As Cumming has commented: 'Not all NGOs enjoy the purest of conceptions.'[50] Indeed, there is increasing evidence of a range of influences on NGOs, not all of which are benign. This reality counteracts a tendency in the scholarship throughout the 1990s and 2000s to deify NGOs. Scholars referred to NGOs' idealism,[51] their adherence to their 'cause' in the face of adversity,[52] and the importance of their moral authority.[53] The

---

49 CERD Committee Member 5, interview conducted Geneva (30 April 2015).
50 Lawrence S Cumming, 'GONGOs' in Helmut Anheier and Stefan Toepler (eds), *International Encyclopedia of Civil Society* (Springer, 2009) 781, 781.
51 Paul Gready (ed), *Fighting for Human Rights* (Routledge, 2004) 28.
52 Kofi Annan, 'Address to the NGOs Forum on Global Issues' (Speech, Berlin, 29 April 1999).
53 Margaret E Keck and Kathryn Sikkink, *Activists Beyond Borders: Advocacy Networks in International Politics* (Cornell University Press, 1998).

title of Willetts' book famously described NGOs as 'the Conscience of the World'.[54] However, grandiose claims about the importance of NGOs have not been uncontested and there has been consistent concern with NGOs' legitimacy and accountability.[55] Of greater concern is the phenomenon of 'fake NGOs', which two of my interviewees alluded to.[56] These are established by Governments to make positive statements about the State's human rights record at the UN.

De Frouville has identified the ever-increasing presence of GONGOs at the UN, which he describes as 'servile NGOs'.[57] He identifies two main categories of GONGO – those which intervene in conflicts between states and the 'laudatory and imitative NGOs'. The latter resonates with the GONGOs described by interviewees for this research. While ECOSOC Resolution 1996/31, which broadened NGO engagement at the UN to include regional and national NGOs, is generally seen as a positive development, de Frouville argues that this was one of the factors which enabled GONGO participation at the UN. A more important question is whether GONGOs are actually influential and effective. They may be particularly problematic in the politicised Human Rights Council environment. Billaud writes that in Venezuela's first Universal Periodic Review by the Council, 80 per cent of 'civil society' contributions came from Communal Councils praising government policies.[58]

Diagram 1 shows how the various types of NGOs typically engage. The arrows indicate that all NGOs must gain access to UN bodies through the international gatekeeper NGO, if one exists. Domestic dependent NGOs are likely to engage with those with more expertise – domestic self-sufficient NGOs and international facilitative NGOs. The dotted line indicates that domestic self-sufficient NGOs may choose to engage with international facilitative NGOs for strategic purposes but are not reliant on them. The

---

54 Peter Willetts (ed), *'The Conscience of the World': The Influence of Non Governmental Organisations in the UN System* (David Davies Memorial Institute of International Studies and the Brookings Institution, 1996).

55 For a succinct summary of the literature, see Kenneth Anderson, 'What NGO Accountability Means – And Does Not Mean' (2009) 103(1) *American Journal of International Law* 170.

56 Treaty body member 2, interview conducted Geneva (28 April 2015) and Government representative 1, member of Human Rights Council, interview conducted Geneva (10 November 2015).

57 Olivier de Frouville, 'Domesticating Civil Society at the United Nations' in *NGOs in International Law* (n 4) 71.

58 Julie Billaud, 'Keepers of the Truth: Producing "Transparent" Documents for the Universal Periodic Review' in Hilary Charlesworth and Emma Larking (eds), *Human Rights and the Universal Periodic Review: Rituals and Ritualism* (Cambridge University Press, 2015) 70.

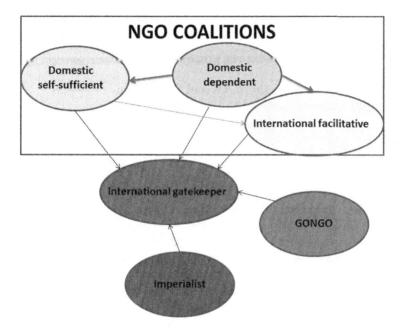

Diagram 1 NGO Taxonomy and Networks

rectangle indicates the most common collaborators in NGO coalitions – various combinations of domestic and international NGOs, with the exception of GONGOs and imperialist NGOs.

In addition to the complexities of defining NGOs, it has also been established that:

> One cannot explain how the United Nations engages with non-state actors in any simple way. There are many parts of the UN with variable autonomy from the rest of the system, and each operates with unique rules governing its relationships with non-state actors. Indeed, the UN is regularly misunderstood in large part because it is particularly difficult to define. It is less a single organization than a loosely integrated system, or 'family' of organizations.[59]

---

59 Molly Ruhlman, *Who Participates in Global Governance? States, Bureaucracies, and NGOs in the United Nations* (Taylor & Francis Group, 2014) 34.

This book navigates this maze by focusing solely on the UN human rights mechanisms and although there remain complexities and idiosyncrasies in how these work, the (formal and informal) methods of engagement and regulation of NGOs for each can be reasonably clearly identified.

4 Previous literature on NGOs and UN human rights bodies

There have been some seminal works on NGOs in the UN human rights system over the years. For example, Korey's 'NGOs and the Universal Declaration of Human Rights: A Curious Grapevine'.[60] But as discussed earlier, it is not uncommon for NGOs to be overlooked in traditional doctrinal scholarship. Where authors have been cognisant that NGOs do play a role, an NGO practitioner is often called upon to write a chapter in an edited book.[61] Broader discussions of the NGO role in international law have also made a useful contribution,[62] as has the field of social sciences,[63] both of which informed this book.

Over the years – and decades – there have been useful examinations of the NGO role in drafting international legislation and bringing individual complaints to treaty bodies,[64] and the role in treaty body State reporting.[65] There was a trend in edited books on human rights whereby academics write the core chapters whilst NGO practitioners provide their perspectives in a stand-alone chapter.[66] There have also been useful studies on the impact of human rights treaties and a body of literature on treaty body reform, although these contain limited analysis of the NGO role.[67]

---

60 William Korey, *NGOs and the Universal Declaration of Human Rights: A Curious Grapevine* (St Martin's Press, 1998).

61 See, e.g. Ben Schokman and Phil Lynch, 'Effective NGO Engagement with the UPR' in Charlesworth and Larking (eds) (n 5) 126; Roland Chauville, 'The UPR's First Cycle: Successes and Failures' in Charlesworth and Larking (eds) (n 58) 87; Andrew Clapham, 'Defining the Role of Non-Governmental Organizations with Regard to the UN Human Rights Treaty Bodies' in Anne F Bayefsky (ed), *The UN Human Rights Treaty System in the 21st Century* (Kluwer Law International, 2000) 183; Rachel Brett, 'The Role of NGOs – An Overview' in Gudmundur Alfredsson et al (eds), *International Human Rights Monitoring Mechanisms Essays in Honour of Jakob Th. Möller* (Martinus Nijhoff, 2nd rev ed, 2009) 673.

62 See, e.g. *NGOs in International Law* (n 4); Lindblom (n 37).

63 See, e.g. Kellow and Murphy-Gregory (eds) (n 15).

64 Cohen (n 8); Pearson (n 8); Hannum (ed) (n 9); Hodson (n 9).

65 Bayefsky (ed) (n 61).

66 Brett (n 61) 673; Clapham (n 61) 183.

67 Christof Heyns and Frans Viljoen, *The Impact of the United Nations Human Rights Treaties on the Domestic Level* (Kluwer Law International, The Netherlands, 2002); University of

Although State-centric theories of international law have been dominant, in the 1990s, international law entered a post-ontological era more open to self-analysis and critique.[68] New ways of thinking about international law, and an openness to the application of social sciences theories and methods to international law emerged at this time.[69] With its emphasis on identifying participants in decision-making, including NGOs,[70] and the perspectives of these actors,[71] the New Haven School paved the way for sociolegal research in international law, such as the research in this book. Concurrently, increasing globalisation posed a challenge to traditional theories of international law.[72]

This era – the 1990s – saw a growth in literature and theories relating to non-State actors and international civil society, including in the area of international law.[73] Post-Cold War, NGOs became more prolific and international human rights laws and monitoring increased, the two being interconnected. Several authors point to the involvement of NGOs in UN human rights world conferences in the 1990s as an important turning point in NGOs' role within the UN system and much of the literature post-dates this.[74] Not only was there high participation by NGOs at such international fora, there were also a significant number of more grassroots level NGOs, rather than international NGOs, for the first time.[75] Several authors have

Nottingham Human Rights Law Centre, *The Dublin Statement on the Process of Strengthening of the United Nations Human Rights Treaty Body System* (2008); Navanetham Pillay, *Strengthening the United Nations Human Rights Treaty Body System: A Report by the United Nations High Commissioner for Human Rights* (Office of the High Commissioner for Human Rights, June 2012).

68 Thomas M Franck, *Fairness in International Law and Institutions* (Oxford University Press, 1995) 6.

69 Harold Hongju Koh, 'Is There a "New" New Haven School of International Law?' (2007) 32(2) *The Yale Journal of International Law* 559.

70 Siegfried Wiessner, 'Legitimacy and Accountability of NGOs: A Policy-Oriented Perspective' in W Michael Reisman et al (eds), *International Law in Contemporary Perspective* (Foundation Press, 2004) 305, 305–11.

71 W Michael Reisman, Siegfried Wiessner and Andrew R Willard, 'The New Haven School: A Brief Introduction' (2007) 32(2) *The Yale Journal of International Law* 575.

72 Pearson (n 8) 92.

73 Holly Cullen and Karen Morrow, 'International Civil Society in International Law: The Growth of NGO Participation' (2001) 1(1) *Non-State Actors and International Law* 7.

74 Jutta M Joachim, *Agenda Setting, the UN, and NGOs: Gender Violence and Reproductive Rights* (Georgetown University Press, 2007); Kerstin Martens, 'NGOs in the United Nations System: Evaluating Theoretical Approaches' (2006) 18(5) *Journal of International Development* 691.

75 Peter Willetts (ed), *'The Conscience of the World': The Influence of Non Governmental Organisations in the UN System* (Brookings Institution Press, 1996) 196.

charted the development of the NGO sector internationally,[76] including the establishment of significant human rights NGOs,[77] and specific achievements of human rights NGOs.[78] Others began to quantify the growth of both international NGOs and later international-facing domestic NGOs.[79]

A trend emerged from the 2000s with some scholars, in their enthusiasm to engage with the topic of NGOs in international human rights law, tending to aggrandise the NGO role. These claims were usually unsupported by empirical evidence. For example, some posited that NGOs played a *significant* role in UN State-reporting mechanisms.[80] Others went further. For example, Forsythe wrote that the NGO role was not just significant, but was in fact essential to State reporting and concluded that when critical questions were asked of governments during reviews, or critical conclusions were reached by UN rapporteurs or committees, it was frequently based on information provided by NGOs.[81] Wiseberg confirmed the essential nature of NGO involvement, making the claim that the UN human rights machinery would grind to a halt without the fact-finding work of NGOs.[82] Egan, writing in 2013, supports the view of Connors, who had described the NGO role in treaty body monitoring as a 'critical dependency'.[83] Yet, as early as 1998, the criticism emerged that research on the significance of NGOs offered little evidence to support claims of success in influencing policy outcomes.[84]

Another challenge to State-centrism is transnationalism,[85] referring to economic, social, and political linkages between people or institutions across the borders of nation-states.[86] Transnational scholarship is relevant to

---

76   Courtney B Smith, *Politics and Process at the United Nations, The Global Dance* (Lynne Rienner Publishers, 2006) 113.

77   Aryeh Neier, *The International Human Rights Movement: A History* (Princeton University Press, 2012).

78   Korey (n 60).

79   Union of International Associations (eds), *Yearbook of International Organizations: Guide to Global Civil Society Networks 2014–2015* (Brill, 2016).

80   In relation to the ICESCR Committee, see, e.g. Freeman(n 2) 152. See generally *Role of NGOs in Protection of Human Rights*(n 2) 350.

81   Forsythe (n 2) 203–4.

82   Wiseberg(n 36) 525.

83   Suzanne Egan, 'Strengthening the United Nations Human Rights Treaty Body System' (2013) 13(2) *Human Rights Law Review* 209, 227.

84   Don Hubert, 'Inferring Influence: Gauging the Impact of NGOs' in Charlotte Ku and Thomas G Weiss (eds), *Toward Understanding Global Governance: The International Law and International Relations Toolbox* (Academic Council on the United Nations System Reports and Papers No. 2, 1998) 27.

85   Linda Camp Keith, 'Human Rights Instruments' in Cane and Kritzer (eds) (n 23) 353, 357.

86   See, e.g. Steven Vertovec, *Transnationalism* (Taylor & Francis Group, 2009).

this book as it includes consideration of the NGO role. Two main branches of transnational theory will be discussed here; firstly, the social sciences-based transnational advocacy networks, and secondly, the law-based theory of transnational legal process.

Key authors such as Keck, Sikkink, Risse (formerly Risse-Kappen), and Ropp argue that international human rights norms are used by networks of transnational and domestic activists and other actors who effectively social-ise States to accept and comply with such norms. Firstly, in the mid-1990s, Risse-Kappen proposed a transnational model to explain NGO behaviour, focusing on international NGOs and networks but with less recognition of domestic NGOs.[87] The focus in the literature on international NGOs and transnational advocacy networks changed as more domestic NGOs were established,[88] and some began to engage with the UN system. Following the transnational model, two subsequent models were significant in academic literature – the spiral model and the boomerang model. First published in 1999, the spiral model still remains influential in human rights research.[89] In the spiral model, diffusing international human rights norms depends on domestic and transnational networks using international regimes to bring issues to the attention of Western governments and citizens.[90]

Keck and Sikkink's boomerang model was perhaps less widely adopted by scholars than the spiral model, but focuses more on the distinctive role of domestic NGOs.[91] It uses the boomerang as a metaphor for the interaction between domestic NGOs and international NGOs, who put pressure on the government in question. Using the boomerang model, networks of transna-tional and domestic NGOs and other actors 'bring pressure "from above" and "from below" to accomplish human rights change'.[92]

The second significant transnational theory of relevance to this book is Koh's transnational legal process theory.[93] Transnational legal process is a

---

87   Thomas Risse-Kappen (ed), *Bringing Transnational Relations Back IN: Non-State Actors, Domestic Structures and International Institutions* (Cambridge University Press, 1995).

88   Union of International Associations (eds) (n 79).

89   See, e.g. Raed A Alhargan, 'The Impact of the UN Human Rights System and Human Rights INGOs on the Saudi Government with Special Reference to the Spiral Model' (2012) 16(4) *The International Journal of Human Rights* 598; Man-Ho Heo, 'Mongolia's Political Change and Human Rights in Five-Phase Spiral Model: Implications for North Korea' (2014) 29(3) *Pacific Focus* 413.

90   Thomas Risse, Stephen C Ropp and Kathryn Sikkink (eds), *The Power of Human Rights, International Norms and Domestic Change* (Cambridge University Press, 1999).

91   Keck and Sikkink (n 53).

92   Thomas Risse and Kathryn Sikkink, 'The Socialization of International Human Rights Norms into Domestic Practices: Introduction' in Risse, Ropp and Sikkink (eds) (n 90) 18.

93   Harold Hongju Koh, 'Transnational Legal Process' (1996) 75 *Nebraska Law Review* 181.

dynamic process by which public and private actors, including States, international organisations, and NGOs, interact in public and private, domestic and international fora to make, interpret, enforce, and internalise rules of international law.[94] Again, this theory departs from previous State-centric theories; Koh identifies the theory as non-traditional and non-Statist.[95]

Koh's perception of the NGO role appears to be solely litigation focused, whereas this book examines the multi-faceted nature of the NGO role. Of relevance here is Koh's analysis of both domestic and international fora, and the actors' role in 'enforcing' and internalising international law. Koh also argues that through a 'repeated process of interaction and internalization' international law acquires its 'stickiness'.[96] The cyclical nature of State reporting to UN treaty bodies and to the Universal Periodic Review is a 'repeated process', for example, and one that NGOs are also heavily engaged with as discussed in Chapters 4 and 5.

Some literature has also questioned underlying assumptions about the concept of global civil society,[97] and the importance of transnational networks. A number of authors acknowledge the importance of *domestic* NGOs and other actors, and the need for international human rights law to be adapted locally. Both Simmons and Merry have proposed that whilst transnational networks may be critical in the case of a repressive regime, in most States, domestic actors are the most significant.[98] Simmons concludes that international human rights treaties are powerful in mobilising domestic NGOs in holding States to account. She argues that this theory is a crucial supplement to existing literature on mechanisms, such as transnational alliances.[99]

Merry finds that NGOs can act as intermediaries so that international law can be adapted as a 'localized globalism'.[100] Some international law scholars had already reached the same general conclusions but without reference to the popular international relations literature described earlier.[101] For example, Heyns and Vilijoen's study of human rights treaty impact on

---

94   Ibid 183–4.

95   Ibid 184.

96   Ibid 198.

97   Daniela Tepe, *The Myth About Global Civil Society: Domestic Politics to Ban Landmines* (Palgrave Macmillan, 2011).

98   Sally Engle Merry, *Human Rights and Gender Violence: Translating International Law into Local Justice* (University of Chicago Press, 2006); Beth Simmons, *Mobilizing for Human Rights: International Law in Domestic Politics* (Cambridge University Press, 2009).

99   Simmons (n 98).

100   Merry (n 98).

101   Role of NGOs in Protection of Human Rights (n 2) 350.

20 States concluded that treaty norms must be internalised in the domestic legal and cultural system by harnessing 'domestic constituencies'.[102]

5 About this book

This book is structured as follows. Chapter 2 discusses the history of the NGO role within the UN human rights system. This is followed by an analysis of the forms and extent of regulation of NGOs in the system in Chapter 3. Chapter 4 then discusses NGO engagement with, and influence on, UN human rights treaties and treaty bodies – effectively the testing ground for the NGO role in the UN human rights system more broadly. This is followed by an analysis of the NGO role in the more recent UN Human Rights Council in Chapter 5. Chapters 4 and 5 are the most substantive and the most practical, containing some of the 'how to' of NGO engagement. They aim to demystify the UN human rights system for NGOs, expose the opportunities available but also analyse the potential for influence to inform NGO strategy. Chapter 6 draws together themes from these chapters and concludes that NGOs play an essential role in UN human rights mechanisms. As heterogeneous actors, the NGO role and influence is multi-faceted, significant, and wide reaching. It includes the provision of expertise, 'on the ground' information, influence on UN recommendations, drafting of instruments, strategic litigation, holding governments to account on their international human rights obligations, and contributing to global governance. In short, their role and influence cannot be over-estimated. As acknowledged by the UN General Assembly:

> The growing participation and influence of non-State actors is enhancing democracy and reshaping multilateralism. Civil society organisations are also the prime movers of some of the most innovative initiatives to deal with emerging global threats.[103]

---

102 Heyns and Viljoen (n 67) 6.
103 A/58/817 General Assembly 11 June 2004 Fifty-eighth session Agenda item 59 Strengthening of the United Nations system, 3.

2 History of the NGO role in the UN human rights system[1]

1 Introduction

'One of the most dramatic transformations in international politics across the last century is the exponential growth in the number of NGOs operating both within and across state borders'.[2] Although NGOs are usually associated with the era from the establishment of the UN, NGOs, or NGO-like organisations, have existed for some time. The history of the development of NGO role is germane to our understanding of NGOs' contemporary role and influence in UN human rights bodies.

Davies argues that the oldest NGOs surviving to the present day are religious establishments, such as the Knights Hospitallier from the eleventh century to which contemporary 'Order of St John' organisations can trace their roots; or the Sufi tariqas of the Islamic world.[3] He notes the small range of 'non-governmental institutions', such as religious orders, missionary groups, charities, scientific societies, and fraternal organisations (e.g. the Freemasons) that existed prior to the late eighteenth century.[4] More cross-border organisations with broader scope emerged during the eighteenth and nineteenth centuries, due to the intellectual, technological, economic, social, and political progress in that period.[5]

---

1 Some of the content of this chapter has been adapted from: Fiona McGaughey, 'The "Curious Grapevine": 70 Years of Non-Governmental Organisations in the United Nations Human Rights System' in Noelle Higgins et al (eds), *The Universal Declaration of Human Rights at Seventy: A Review of Successes and Challenges* (Clarus Press Ltd, 2020) ('Curious Grapevine').

2 Courtney B Smith, *Politics and Process at the United Nations, the Global Dance* (Lynne Rienner Publishers, 2006) 111.

3 Thomas Davies, 'The Historical Development of NGOs' in Aynsley Kellow and Hannah Murphy-Gregory (eds), *Handbook of Research on NGOs* (Edward Elgar Publishing, 2018) 15–6.

4 Ibid 16.

5 Ibid, 16–7.

The late nineteenth century then saw a rapid period of expansion of transnational NGOs with more formalised structures, many of which still exist today.[6] These include the World Alliance of Young Men's Christian Associations established in 1855, the International Committee of the Red Cross established in 1863, and the International Council of Women established in 1888. The 1900s saw the creation of many NGOs across a range of areas of interest, including the Union of International Associations, aimed at representing all international associations in a Federated body.[7] Both world wars inevitably saw an initial contraction of European-based NGOs, later followed by the establishment of humanitarian and peace-focused NGOs.[8]

The creation of the League of Nations presented the first real opportunity for NGO engagement with an international organisation and as discussed in the next section, the NGO role at the UN led on from the civil society engagement that had been established in the League of Nations.

At the 50th anniversary of the Universal Declaration of Human Rights (UDHR), then Secretary General, Kofi Annan, stated:

> Before the founding of the United Nations, NGOs led the charge in the adoption of some of the Declaration's forerunners. The Geneva conventions of 1864; multilateral labour conventions adopted in 1906; and the International Slavery Convention of 1926; all stemmed from the world of NGOs who infused the international community with a spirit of reform.[9]

Therefore, NGOs – albeit perhaps less commonly called 'NGOs' at that time – had been in existence and active for some time. Historical civil society engagement has been documented with regard to international campaigns against slavery and trafficking, notably The Anti-Slavery Society, and in the development of standards of international humanitarian law by the International Committee of the Red Cross.[10] The International Association for Labour Legislation was instrumental in the conclusion of international labour conventions in 1905, 1906, and 1913, which paved the way

---

6 Ibid, 18.

7 Ibid, 19.

8 Ibid, 20–2.

9 Kofi Annan, 'Address to the 51st Annual DPI-NGO Conference' (Speech, United Nations, 1998).

10 Theo van Boven, 'The Role of Non-Governmental Organizations in International Human Rights Standard-Setting: A Prerequisite of Democracy' (1990) 20(2) *California Western International Law Journal* 207, 209.

for many conventions later adopted by the International Labour Organization (ILO).[11]

The remainder of this chapter charts the development of the role and influence of NGOs at the UN. This influence began with their role in the drafting of the UN Charter, ensuring the inclusion of human rights provisions in the Charter – without which the entire UN human rights system might not exist – and ensuring a role for NGOs in the Charter through Article 71 which provided for consultation with NGOs. Substantial engagement of NGOs and opportunities for NGO influence in UN human rights bodies began with their engagement with treaty bodies, the Commission, and then the Human Rights Council (HRC), each of which is explored here. We begin by examining the early era of the UN and the not insignificant NGO engagement and influence at that time.

2 NGOs before, and in the early years of the UN

The existence of NGOs and their advocacy role with international organisations prior to the establishment of the UN is evident from the engagement of NGOs with its predecessor, the League of Nations ('the League'). The Covenant establishing the League had limited provisions on NGOs, such as Article 25 on creating national Red Cross organisations.[12] Informally though, NGOs were well recognised by the League, invited to sit on selected committees (although without voting rights), and to attend meetings.[13] There was a more strained relationship between the League and NGOs later in the League's existence, which is one possible explanation for the initial relative lack of engagement with NGOs in the lead-up to the establishment of the UN.

Paragraph 4 of the Moscow Declaration of 1943 recognised the need for a post-war international organisation to replace the League and the Dumbarton Oaks Conference of 1944 was the first step towards this. The conference resulted in proposals for the new organisation which would become the UN but did not include provisions for an NGO role. This omission was subsequently addressed by NGOs at the San Francisco Conference in 1945 where there were an estimated 1,200 'voluntary

---

11   Ibid 210.

12   *Treaty of Versailles*, signed 28 June 1919 (entered into force 10 January 1920) Pt 1 (Covenant of the League of Nations).

13   Steve Charnovitz, 'Two Centuries of Participation: NGOs and International Governance' (1997) 18(2) *Michigan Journal of International* Law 183, 221.

organisations' in attendance,[14] many of whom were part of state delegations.[15] These organisations, which we now refer to as NGOs, were active contributors to the drafting of the Charter,[16] including the drafting of Article 71, which provides that the Economic and Social Council (ECOSOC):

> may make suitable arrangements for consultation with non-governmental organizations which are concerned with matters within its competence. Such arrangements may be made with international organizations and, where appropriate, with national organizations after consultation with the Member of the United Nations concerned.[17]

The inclusion of Article 71 is significant as it provides the legal basis for the NGO role in the UN and it has been suggested that the term 'non-governmental organization' was effectively coined at this time. The acceptance of Article 71 in the drafting of the Charter was due to the influence of NGOs but also of the Soviet Union which sought a status for the World Federation of Trade Unions (WFTU). The WFTU was, to some extent, under Soviet influence.[18] Article 71 is sometimes heralded as a revolutionary hard law provision for an NGO role. However, Otto argues that it simply formalised the extensive NGO consultative relationships which had existed in the League.[19] In fact, Article 71 was more restrictive than practices at the League as it limited NGO input to economic and social matters but not matters of more significance, such as international peace and security.[20] Confining UN consultation with NGOs to the remit of ECOSOC was also seen as a way to limit the influence of NGOs due to ECOSOC's relative lack of power as an organ of the UN (compared with the General Assembly

---

14 Chadwick Alger, 'The Emerging Roles of NGOs in the UN System: From Article 71 to a People's Millennium Assembly' (2002) 8(1) *Global Governance* 93, 93. See also, Pei-Heng Chiang, *Non-Governmental Organisations at the United Nations – Identity, Role and Function* (Frederick A Praeger, 1981).

15 Bob Reinalda, 'NGOs in the History of Intergovernmental Organizations' in Kellow and Murphy-Gregory (eds) (n 3) 35, 47.

16 Ibid.

17 *Charter of the United Nations*, signed 26 June 1945, 1 UNTS XVI (entered into force 24 October 1945) art 71.

18 Reinalda (n 15) 48.

19 Dianne Otto, 'Nongovernmental Organizations in the United Nations System: The Emerging Role of International Civil Society' (1996) 18(1) *Human Rights Quarterly* 107, 109.

20 Reinalda (n 15) 47.

or Security Council).[21] Willetts argues that the term 'consultative status' was deliberately chosen to indicate a secondary role involving provision of advice but not active participation in the decision-making process.[22]

Another significant NGO contribution to the drafting of the UN Charter was successfully lobbying for human rights to be included.[23] Van Boven writes that at a crucial stage of the San Francisco conference, it became clear that the draft Charter lacked human rights protections and so a delegation of NGO representatives 'carried out an urgent demarche with US Secretary of State Stettinius'.[24] They persuaded him that the US needed to take action to strengthen the Charter in the area of human rights, reporting that this view 'reflected fundamental desires of the vast majority of people'.[25] Their lobbying was successful and reported by Secretary of State Stettinius to President Truman:

> In no part of the deliberations of the Conference was greater interest displayed than by the group of American consultants representing forty-two leading American organizations and groups concerned with the enjoyment of human rights and basic freedoms to all peoples. . . . A direct outgrowth of discussions between the United States delegation and the Consultants was the proposal of the United States delegation in which it was joined by other sponsoring powers that the Charter [Article 68] be amended to provide for a Commission on Human Rights.[26]

It is interesting that the Secretary of State described the delegation as 'consultants' representing 'organisations and groups concerned with the enjoyment of human rights', reaffirming the hypothesis that the language of 'non-governmental organization' which was subsequently used in the Charter, was not yet well established at this time. Again, like Article 71, this is a very significant inclusion in the Charter and as well as providing for the establishment of a Commission on Human Rights, the phrase 'human rights' was eventually used seven times in the Charter. Had human rights been absent from the Charter, there would have been no legal foundation for our current UN human rights laws and institutions.

21 Douglas Williams, *The Specialized Agencies and the United Nations: The System in Crisis* (Hurst, 1987) 260–1.
22 Peter Willetts, 'From "Consultative Arrangements" to "Partnership": The Changing Status of NGOs in Diplomacy at the UN' (2000) 6(2) *Global Governance* 191, 191.
23 Alger (n 14) 93.
24 van Boven (n 10) 210.
25 Ibid.
26 Ibid.

3 Expanding human rights themes and instruments – the NGO contribution

Building on their success in influencing the drafting of the Charter, NGOs were actively engaged in the drafting of the UDHR. The significance of their influence is well established by Korey in his book 'NGOs and the Universal Declaration of Human Rights: A Curious Grapevine'.[27] Van Boven notes that NGO participation in the UDHR drafting process was dominated by Western NGOs, including representatives of Jewish and Christian organisations.[28] For example, Article 16 of the UDHR on the Rights of the Family was influenced by Catholic groups and Article 18 on Freedom of Religion is often attributed to Dr. Nolde, former Director of the Commission of the Churches on International Affairs of the World Council of Churches.[29] Given the influence of NGOs in the drafting, it is perhaps unsurprising that Eleanor Roosevelt, who chaired the UDHR working group, predicted the importance of the NGO role. She famously stated that the rights in the UDHR would become known through a 'curious grapevine', namely NGOs.[30]

In 1968, ECOSOC Resolution 1296 *Arrangements for Consultation with Non-governmental Organizations* was adopted.[31] The adoption and amendment of consultative arrangements on a number of occasions, and the implications for the NGO role and influence, is discussed further in Chapter 3. In this same era, following their participation in the drafting of the UDHR, there was active, albeit informal, participation by NGOs in the drafting of the International Covenant on Civil and Political Rights ('ICCPR')[32] and the International Covenant on Economic Social and Cultural Rights ('ICESCR')[33] where NGOs lobbied government representatives with their suggestions. During the drafting of the ICCPR and ICESCR, Malik noted: 'the non-governmental organizations . . . served as batteries of unofficial advisers to the various delegations, supplying them with streams of ideas

---

27 William Korey, *NGOs and the Universal Declaration of Human Rights: A Curious Grapevine* (Palgrave McMillan, 1998).

28 van Boven (n 10) 211.

29 Ibid.

30 See, e.g. Korey (n 27).

31 *Arrangements for Consultation with Non-Governmental Organizations*, ESC December 1296 (XLVI), UN ESCOR, 1528th plen mtg, UN Doc E/RES/1296(XLVI) (29 May 1968).

32 *International Covenant on Civil and Political Rights*, opened for signature 16 December 1966, 999 UNTS 171 (entered into force 23 March 1976) ('ICCPR').

33 *International Covenant on Economic, Social and Cultural Rights,* opened for signature 16 December 1966, 993 UNTS 3 (entered into force 3 January 1976) ('ICESCR').

and suggestions'.[34] However, their influence did not stretch as far as formal provisions for an NGO role in either the ICCPR or ICESCR treaty.

It has been noted that Western NGOs were more actively engaged in the drafting of the international Bill of Rights (the UDHR, ICCPR and ICESCR) than NGOs from other global regions.[35] As well as the ubiquitous Western bias in international law generally,[36] a particular gap earlier in the UN history was specific recognition of and protection for the rights of Indigenous peoples. This only shifted following the 'Study of the Problem of Discrimination against Indigenous Populations' by Mr. Jose Martinez Cobo, Special Rapporteur of the Sub-Commission on Prevention of Discrimination and Protection of Minorities ('the Cobo Report').[37] Recommendations from the Cobo Report, of particular relevance to this book, included options for Indigenous peoples' representation at the UN. In 1982, based on these recommendations and as a result of the growing advocacy of Indigenous and non-Indigenous NGOs, ECOSOC authorised the establishment of the UN Working Group on Indigenous Populations (WGIP).[38]

These developments, their broader implications and their effectiveness, have also been subject to critique. For example, Corntassel reviewed Indigenous participation in the WGIP and Permanent Forum on Indigenous Issues and concluded that these fora can 'blunt' or 'tame' Indigenous agendas of self-determination and pursuit of justice.[39] In fact, he posits that Indigenous people risk becoming 'co-opted' for the benefit of the UN – but not always for the benefit of their own community. Morgan has charted the development of the global Indigenous movement and argues that activities over the past few decades in particular have led to a high level of international recognition and responsiveness for Indigenous advocates, the adoption of new

---

34 Otto Frederick Nolde, *Free and Equal: Human Rights in Ecumenical Perspective, with Reflections on the Origin of the Universal Declaration of Human Rights by Charles Habib Malik* (World Council of Churches, 1968) 21–4, cited in van Boven (n 10) 211.

35 Marc J Bossuyt, *Guide to the "Travaux Preparatoires" of the International Covenant on Civil and Political Rights* (Martinus Nijhoff Publishers, 1987) 823.

36 See, e.g. Irene Watson, 'Aboriginal(ising) International Law and Other Centres of Power' (2011) 20(3) *Griffith Law Review* 619; Makau Mutua, 'What Is TWAIL?' (2000) 94 *Proceedings of the Annual Meeting; American Society of International Law* 31.

37 van Boven (n 10) 216; Rhiannon Morgan, *Transforming Law and Institution: Indigenous Peoples, the United Nations and Human Rights* (Routledge, 2011) 20.

38 Morgan (n 37) 20.

39 Jeff Corntassel, 'Partnership in Action? Indigenous Political Mobilization and Co-Optation During the First UN Indigenous Decade (1994–2004)' (2007) 29(1) *Human Rights Quarterly* 137.

standards, the establishment of innovative spaces for representation, and an impetus to mainstream Indigenous issues across the UN.[40] Conversely, she is not convinced that this has always led to improvements on the ground, as Indigenous peoples worldwide 'continue to live in conditions of extreme disadvantage and to experience pervasive and prejudicial threats to their continued existence and ways of life from states, multinationals, rebels, and other harmful agents'.[41]

The importance of consultation with, and participation of, Indigenous peoples at the UN has been supported several times since,[42] including in the 2017 UN General Assembly resolution: *Enhancing the participation of Indigenous peoples' representatives and institutions in meetings of relevant United Nations bodies on issues affecting them.*[43]

In terms of other human rights agendas that were furthered by NGOs, Van Boven notes that NGOs were particularly instrumental with regard to prevention of torture and the rights of prisoners and detainees.[44] The 1960s and 1970s saw the establishment of some of the most high-profile human rights NGOs, such as Amnesty International and Human Rights Watch.[45] Van Boven credits Amnesty International's 1972 campaign for the Abolition of Torture – along with broader contextual issues, such as the military coup d'état and associated acts of brutality in Chile in 1973 – as raising public and governmental awareness of torture.[46] This led to a sustained focus on the protection of persons subjected to detention or imprisonment, originating in the UN General Assembly in 1973. A number of international instruments were subsequently adopted, most notably the Convention against Torture and Other Cruel, Inhuman or Degrading Treatment or Punishment in 1984, and several NGOs, including the International Commission of Jurists and

---

40 Morgan (n 37) 131.

41 Ibid 132.

42 *UN Declaration on the Rights of Indigenous People*, GA Res 61/295, UN GAOR, 61st sess, Agenda Item 68, UN Doc A/RES/61/295 (2 October 2007, adopted 13 September 2007).

43 *Enhancing the Participation of Indigenous Peoples' Representatives and Institutions in Meetings of Relevant United Nations Bodies on Issues Affecting Them*, GA Res 71/321, UN GAOR, 71st sess, Agenda Item 65, UN Doc A/RES/71/321 (21 September 2017, adopted 8 September 2017).

44 van Boven (n 10) 213. See also, V. Leary, 'A New Role for Non-Governmental Organizations in Human Rights: A Case Study of Non-Governmental Participation in the Development of International Norms on Torture' in Antonio Cassese (ed), *UN Law/Fundamental Rights: Two Topics In International Law* (Sijthoff & Noordhoff, 1979) 197.

45 Aryeh Neier, *The International Human Rights Movement: A History* (Princeton University Press, 2012).

46 van Boven (n 10) 213.

Amnesty International made significant contributions to the drafting of the various legal instruments.[47]

As discussed further in Chapter 4, over the years NGOs became increasingly active in the drafting of treaties, in particular the Convention on the Rights of the Child (CRoC).[48] Van Boven reports that this drafting process mobilised numerous NGOs and that 35 organisations established an informal 'NGO Ad Hoc Group' in Geneva to develop common approaches and strategies regarding CRoC.[49] He notes that many articles of the draft convention adopted by UN General Assembly in 1989 were proposed or influenced by NGOs.[50]

During the 1990s, the number of NGOs increased significantly, coinciding with the adoption of the new UN human rights treaties some NGOs had been involved in drafting – and the associated monitoring opportunities for NGOs. The treaties provided an impetus for NGOs to engage with the newly formed monitoring 'treaty bodies' or committees.

4 The development of the NGO role in UN human rights treaty body reporting

From the 1970s, NGOs began carving out a role for themselves in contributing to the State-reporting process of the new UN human rights treaty bodies. They began by contributing information to the treaty bodies in order to inform reviews of States' compliance with their human rights obligations under each treaty. Each of the UN's nine core human rights treaties has its own Committee to monitor implementation of the treaty among States parties, primarily through considering periodic reports.[51] It is an often overlooked fact that the International Convention on the Elimination of Racial Discrimination (ICERD)[52] is the longest standing of the UN human rights treaties, having been adopted before both the ICCPR and the ICESCR. ICERD entered into force in 1969 and the CERD Committee began its work

---

47 *International Convention against Torture and Other Cruel, Inhuman and Degrading Treatment or Punishment*, opened for signature 10 December 1984, 1465 UNTS 85 (entered into force 26 June 1987).

48 *Convention on the Rights of the Child*, opened for signature 20 November 1989, 1577 UNTS 3 (entered into force 2 September 1990).

49 van Boven (n 10) 215.

50 Ibid.

51 The terms UN Committee and treaty body are both used here, with the same meaning.

52 *International Convention on the Elimination of All Forms of Racial Discrimination*, opened for signature 21 December 1965, 660 UNTS 195 (entered into force 4 January 1969) ('ICERD').

in 1970, leading the way for the drafting and operation of future human rights treaties. As discussed here, the CERD Committee was the testing ground for NGO involvement in State reporting.

In those early days, some CERD Committee members were resistant to NGO involvement – they were keen to preserve State sovereignty and to avoid 'interfering' in the internal affairs of the States parties.[53] To provide clarity, in 1972 the Chair of the Committee concluded 'it appears . . . that the Committee would continue the practice it had followed to date, allowing members to use any information they might have as experts'.[54] Therefore, the use of unofficial information, such as NGO reports, was considered valid for those Committee members who wished to use it. The weakening of resistance to NGO involvement was bolstered in 1974. At the request of the CERD Committee, the UN Office of Legal Affairs advised that ICERD did not specify which sources the Committee would use, leaving it open for the Committee to use unofficial material from NGOs.[55] The use of NGO reports by the CERD Committee or other treaty bodies has been challenged by governments a number of times since, albeit unsuccessfully.[56] For example, in 2011, UN proposals to align interaction of treaty bodies with governments, NGOs, and National Human Rights Institutions, as part of the treaty body strengthening process,[57] were vehemently rejected by some States who sought to use the opportunity to reduce the NGO role.[58]

While NGO engagement was being tested by the CERD Committee, other treaty bodies were being established. A former employee of Amnesty International recalls that when the Human Rights Committee (which monitors the ICCPR) was established in the mid-1970s, it was 'a contentious issue whether

---

53 Felice D Gaer, 'Implementing International Human Rights Norms: UN Human Rights Treaty Bodies and NGOs' (2003) 2(3) *Journal of Human Rights* 339.

54 Ibid 343.

55 Ibid 342.

56 Ibid 342–3.

57 Office of the High Commissioner for Human Rights, *Non-Exhaustive List of Emerging Proposals Identified So Far in the Context of the Treaty Body Strengthening Informal Consultations (including Dublin, Marrakesh, Poznan, Sion, Seoul, Pretoria, Bristol and Lucerne) and Those of the Inter-Committee Meeting (ICM) and Meeting of Chairpersons (MC), as well as Other Proposals Stemming from the Process* (9 November 2011) <http://www2.ohchr.org/english/bodies/HRTD/docs/ProposalsTBStrengtheningProcess.pdf>.

58 See, e.g. submissions on the matter from China, Russia and Egypt: Government of China, *Views of the Chinese Government Regarding the Human Rights Treaty Body Strengthening Process*, UN Doc HRC/NONE/2011/184 (2011) para 2.6; Government of the Russian Federation, *Comments of the Russian Federation on the List of Issues Identified During the Treaty Body Strengthening Consultations, Prepared by the Office of the United Nations High Commissioner for Human Rights*, UN Doc HRC/NONE/2012/1 (2011) para 2; Government of Egypt, *The Future of the Treaty Body System: Egypt Position Paper* 3.

NGOs could play any role' regarding their work.[59] Gaer reports that at that time, any documents from NGOs had to be delivered in sealed envelopes addressed to each member of the Human Rights Committee, so that the Secretariat would not be seen to disseminate unofficial documents. This practice changed as individual treaty body members expressed the need for alternative sources of information independent of the government reports; meanwhile, human rights NGOs became more professionalised and had capacity to provide reliable factual data as well as international and local expertise.[60] Other treaty bodies began with a similar practice until gradually use of NGO information became more widespread and accepted. In the 1990s, NGOs submitting reports and information to treaty bodies became more common and the OHCHR through its Secretariats began to provide support for this function.[61]

The increased NGO participation and importance of NGO information also began to receive formal acknowledgement from treaty bodies. For example, it was first noted by the CERD Committee in its annual report to the General Assembly in 1996 that NGO commentaries 'complemented the information available to members and helped improve the quality of the Committee's examination of those reports'.[62] Therefore by 1996, NGOs had become important to the CERD Committee and it adopted general guidelines for interacting with NGOs.[63] Gaer reports that during the 1990s, reports from the coordination meetings of Chairpersons of the (then) six core UN human rights treaty bodies repeatedly affirmed the important, 'valuable', 'vital', and 'central' role played by NGOs as reliable sources of independent information for treaty bodies.[64] As discussed in Chapter 4, today all treaty bodies engage with NGOs in broadly similar ways – with some minor variations, such as the role for NGOs in Article 45 (a) of the *Convention on the Rights of the Child*, which provides that the Committee 'may invite . . . other competent bodies as it may consider appropriate to provide expert advice on the implementation of the Convention in areas falling within the scope of their respective mandates'.[65] The Chairs of the Committees co-operate with

59 Gaer (n 53) 343.
60 Ibid.
61 See, e.g. Lena J Kruckenberg, *The UNreal World of Human Rights: An Ethnography of the UN Committee on the Elimination of Racial Discrimination* (Nomos Publishers, 2012).
62 United Nations Committee on the Elimination of Racial Discrimination, *Report of the Committee on the Elimination of Racial Discrimination*, UN GAOR, 51st sess, Supp No 18, UN Doc A/51/18 (30 September 1996) viii.
63 Kruckenberg (n 61) ch 5:2.
64 Gaer (n 53) 345.
65 The Committee's rules confirm that 'other competent bodies' includes NGOs: Committee on the Rights of the Child, *Provisional Rules of Procedure*, UN Doc CRC/C/4 (14 November 1991) rules 34, 70, 74.

each other and the UN is working towards more simplified reporting with common working methods among the Committees.[66]

In the 2000s, some treaty bodies began to hold a weekly briefing with NGOs from all States being reviewed in a given week.[67] The reform of treaty bodies, or 'treaty body strengthening process' from 2009 to 2014 resulted in GA Resolution 68/268 (2014),[68] and drove additional pressure to engage in a more structured way with NGOs.[69]

5 The development of the NGO role in the Commission and Human Rights Council

The Commission on Human Rights was a significant site for the development of the NGO role and opportunities for influence. Lauren argues:

> That is, the Commission did more than any other body within the United Nations to open its deliberations to and invite comments from human rights NGOs. Although the Charter spoke in glowing terms about 'we the peoples,' it often appeared as though only the Commission on Human Rights took the charge seriously. Through time, the majority of members came to view NGOs as effective partners in promoting human rights and thus gave them access and recognized status to constructively engage in presenting evidence of violations by governments against their own people, representing elements of larger civil society, speaking truth to power, and giving voice to voiceless victims.[70]

A significant opportunity for NGO engagement with the Commission arose in 1970 when, despite enormous opposition from governments, it was decided that the Commission could hear complaints from individuals, groups, or NGOs related to widespread patterns of gross violations of

---

66 Navanetham Pillay, *Strengthening the United Nations Human Rights Treaty Body System: A Report by the United Nations High Commissioner for Human Rights* (Office of the High Commissioner for Human Rights, June 2012).

67 See, e.g. *Report of the Committee on the Elimination of Racial Discrimination: Eightieth Session,* UN GAOR, 67th sess, Supp No 18, UN Doc A/67/18(13 February – 9 March 2012), para 65.

68 *Strengthening and Enhancing the Effective Functioning of the Human Rights Treaty Body System,* GA Res 68/268, UN GAOR, 68th sess, Agenda Item 125, UN Doc A/RES/68/268 (21 April 2014, adopted 9 April 2014).

69 Curious Grapevine (n 1).

70 Paul Gordon Lauren, '"To Preserve and Build on its Achievements and to Redress its Shortcomings": The Journey from the Commission on Human Rights to the Human Rights Council' 2007 29(2) *Human Rights Quarterly* 307, 324.

human rights.[71] Some States such as Iran, Cuba, and the Philippines tried to resist and then undermine this, but letter-writing campaigns and information gathering by NGOs attracted considerable international attention to a number of serious, high profile situations.[72]

Over time, the Commission's annual sessions began to bring hundreds of people together in one room, including State representatives, survivors of human rights abuses, and 'NGOs trying to find a seat or a place just to stand in the packed room'.[73] This served to produce a strong panopticon effect whereby State delegations felt under international scrutiny from both States and NGOs. The Commission also supported the World Conference on Human Rights in 1993, which attracted over 2,000 delegates and almost 4,000 NGO representatives, resulting in the Vienna Declaration and Program of Action which asserted that all human rights represented a legitimate international concern.[74] Not only was there high participation by NGOs overall, in this and other World Conferences in the 1990s, there were also a significant number of grassroots level NGOs, rather than international NGOs, for the first time.[75]

The 1990s therefore was a period of burgeoning for NGOs. Bloodgood has rightly identified the challenges and risks of attempts to quantify NGOs, including differences in definitions, information sources, and methodological questions of comparability and generalisability.[76] The following comments are made with this qualifier in mind. Certainly the number of what we now refer to as NGOs appears to have been lower before the UN was established. For example, Smith reports that there were approximately 330 international NGOs in 1914, rising to 2,300 NGOs by 1970.[77] In 1948, only 41 NGOs held consultative status with ECOSOC, but this increased to 500 by 1968 and to 2,000 by 1992.[78] As of April 2020, there are 5,451 NGOs in consultative status with ECOSOC.[79] However, not all NGOs engaged

71 *Procedure for Dealing with Communications Relating to Violations of Human Rights and Fundamental Freedoms*, ESC Dec 1503 (XLVII), UN ESCOR, 1693rd plen mtg, UN Doc E/RES/1503(XLVII) (27 May 1970).

72 Lauren (n 70) 324.

73 Ibid 325.

74 Ibid 324.

75 Willetts (n 22) 196.

76 Elizabeth Bloodgood, 'Quantifying NGOs' in Kellow and Murphy-Gregory (eds) (n 3) 114.

77 Smith (n 2) 113.

78 John Humphrey, 'The UN Charter and the Universal Declaration of Human Rights' in Evan Luard (ed), *The International Protection of Human Rights* (Frederick A Praeger, 1967) 39–40, cited in Korey (n 27) 2.

79 'Basic Facts about ECOSOC Status' *NGO Branch: Department of Economic and Social Affairs* (Web Page) <https://csonet.org/?menu=100>.

in human rights work are in consultative status with ECOSOC. For example, Smith notes that by 2017, there were 69,282 international non-profit organisations, including national NGOs with an international focus.[80] She attributes the rapid increase in NGOs to three things – the rise of new actors and issues on the international agenda post-Cold War, developments in technology that enabled information exchange and travel, and the increased resources available to NGOs.[81] Davies notes that this trajectory of growth has not always been steady and that there have also been periods of contraction over the years.[82]

Several authors point to the high-profile involvement of NGOs in UN human rights world conferences in the 1990s as an important turning point in NGOs' role within the UN system.[83] Alger reflects that these UN world conferences inspired NGOs to host their own conferences, including follow-ups to UN world conferences and NGO conferences with broader agendas, such as one dedicated to the development of effective NGO strategies for engagement in the UN system, and another on the role of NGOs in the twenty-first century.[84] Of particular note was 'the People's Millennium Forum', held in parallel with the 55th session of the UN General Assembly (the Millennium Assembly).[85]

In 2000, the Millennium Declaration committed to 'give greater opportunities to the private sector, non-governmental organizations and civil society, in general, to contribute to the realization of the Organization's goals and programmes'.[86] In 2003 Kofi Annan established a panel of 'eminent persons to review the relationship between the United Nations and civil society'. The Chair was Fernando Henrique Cardoso, the former president of Brazil, and the subsequent report became known as the 'Cardoso Report'.[87] The report acknowledged that governments do not always welcome the participation of NGOs but strongly supported 'civil society' participation. It stated that constructively engaging with civil society is a *necessity* for the UN, not an option.[88]

---

80 *Brill Yearbook of International Organizations* (Web Page) <http://ybio.brillonline.com/ybio/>

81 Smith (n 2) 112.

82 Davies (n 3).

83 Willetts (n 22) 194.

84 Alger (n 14) 115.

85 Ibid.

86 *Strengthening of the United Nations System*, 58th sess, Agenda Item 59, UN Doc A/58/817 (11 June 2004).

87 *We the Peoples: Civil Society, the United Nations and Global Governance: Report of the Panel of Eminent Persons on United Nations – Civil Society Relations*, UN GAOR, 58th sess, Agenda Item 59, UN Doc A/58/817 (11 June 2004).

88 Ibid.

Also around this time, tensions and strains between the Commission and NGOs were common. For example, in 2003 Libya was elected to chair the Commission despite Gaddafi's dictatorship routinely abusing human rights. NGOs protested to no avail and NGO 'Reporters Without Borders' declared: 'By putting Libya at the helm, the commission shows that it is ready to cover up the brutalities of some of its members through dirty deals'.[89] Of course this politicisation of the Commission was ultimately part of its downfall. According to Tistounet, the Commission's credibility and professionalism was eroded by 'ideological confrontation, double standards, selectivity and hidden political agendas exercised in addressing human rights issues'.[90] Specific issues included prioritising civil and political rights to the detriment of economic, social, and cultural rights, and the right to development; and the manipulation of human rights for political ends by using country-specific resolutions.[91]

Politicisation was not the sole domain of States however. As discussed in Chapter 1, there are a variety of types of NGOs, including some that are close to Governments, if not in fact GONGOs. With regard to the Commission, De Frouville explored the engagement of servile NGOs, namely those which appear to be 'serving' the State.[92] He found evidence of NGOs operating in situations of conflict between two States whereby they would discredit the other State by accusing it of human rights violations and serve their own State by praising its human rights progress. He illustrates this by drawing on the relationship between the US and Cuba, and the conflict between India and Pakistan over Kashmir.[93] Such behaviour tarnishes the reputation of the many, independent NGOs – each with their own agendas – but which do not engage in such preferential treatment. This behaviour has also led to calls for better regulation of NGO engagement at the UN, as discussed in Chapter 3.

UN Secretary-General Kofi Annan's 2005 report 'In Larger Freedom: Towards Development, Security, and Human Rights for All'[94] laid out the

---

89   Lauren (n 70) 328.

90   Eric Tistounet, 'From Commission on Human Rights to Human Rights Council: Itinerary of a Reform Process' in Walter Kälin et al (eds), *International Law, Conflict and Development: The Emergence of a Holistic Approach in International Affairs* (Brill | Nijhoff, 2010) 325, 330.

91   Ibid, 330–1.

92   Olivier De Frouville, 'Domesticating Civil Society at the United Nations' in Pierre-Marie Dupuy and Luisa Vierucci (eds), *NGOs in International Law: Efficiency in Flexibility* (Edward Elgar Publishing, 2008) 71, 73.

93   Ibid 73–8.

94   UN Secretary General, *In Larger Freedom: Development, Security, and respect for Human Rights*, General Assembly 59th Sess. UN Doc A/59/2005 (26 May 2005).

need for reform, the demise of the Commission, and a proposed Human Rights Council as a replacement. His proposal included considering whether the Council would be a principal organ of the UN or a subsidiary body of the General Assembly, both of which elevated the status from that of the Commission, which was a subsidiary of ECOSOC. Members would be elected by the General Assembly by a two-thirds majority of members present and voting through secret ballot and those elected to the Council should undertake to abide by the highest human rights standards. NGOs were stunned, but pleased with his bold, transformative proposed reforms.[95] Following extensive negotiations and lobbying, in which NGOs played an important role,[96] the new Human Rights Council ('the Council') was established by resolution 60/251 in 2006 to replace the UN Commission on Human Rights,[97] and as a subsidiary of the General Assembly. In general, the new procedures and standards were welcomed by NGOs.[98]

However, as a political body, the Council has also been accused of political bias and politicisation,[99] although not to the same extent as the Commission. Freedman and Houghton argue that treatment of NGOs at the Council is evidence of this politicisation, particularly those NGOs raising concerns regarding the human rights records of dominant states, such as the International Service for Human Rights' attempts to draw attention to reprisals against a human rights defender in China.[100] Barriers faced by NGOs at the Council include being denied accreditation, ignored within Council sessions, and having their participation challenged by states. Freedman and Houghton conclude that 'NGO participation is another area where in theory there is progress, but in practice, the politicisation of NGO accreditation and proceedings has threatened their inclusion at the Council'.[101] The current operations of the Council and NGO engagement and influence are discussed further in Chapter 5.

---

95 Lauren (n 70) 331.

96 Ibid 334.

97 *Human Rights Council*, GA Res 60/251, UN GAOR, 60th sess, Agenda Items 46 and 120, UN Doc A/RES/60/251 (3 April 2006, adopted 15 March 2006).

98 Lauren (n 70) 341.

99 See, e.g. Edward R McMahon, *Herding Cats and Sheep: Assessing State and Regional Behavior in the Universal Periodic Review Mechanism of the United Nations Human Rights Council* (University of Vermont, July 2010); Rochelle Terman and Erik Voeten, 'The Relational Politics of Shame: Evidence from the Universal Periodic Review' (2018) 13(1) *The Review of International Organizations* 1; Rosa Freedman and Ruth Houghton, 'Two Steps Forward, One Step Back: Politicisation of the Human Rights Council' (2017) 17(4) *Human Rights Law Review* 753.

100 Freedman and Houghton (n 99) 755.

101 Ibid 762.

6 Conclusion

Although non-governmental groups, charities, church groups, and other societal groups have existed for many years, the term 'NGO' only became common in the post-World War II era. NGOs have become significant actors in the UN human rights system, but as discussed here, this was not necessarily an inevitable conclusion. They were initially absent from the UN Charter until they successfully lobbied for inclusion – and lobbied for human rights principles in the Charter. This initial, limited consultative role under Article 71 of the Charter then gradually expanded over the years, although not necessarily in a linear way as States often resisted NGO influence. By contributing expertise to the drafting of international instruments, including the Charter, the UDHR, and human rights treaties, and by identifying opportunities created by the suite of UN human rights treaties, NGOs crafted a role for themselves, increasing in both numbers and influence.

3 UN regulation of NGOs

1 Introduction

The previous chapter mapped the development of the NGO role and influence from the time of the UN Charter onwards. Concomitantly, the regulation of NGOs, primarily through ECOSOC, was developed and refined. As discussed in the previous chapters, Article 71 of the Charter was significant in establishing a formal role for NGOs in the newly established UN. Specifically, it provided for 'consultation' and resulted in the establishment of an accreditation system, discussed in this chapter. This remains the only formal NGO accreditation mechanism for NGOs engaging with UN human rights bodies. However, drawing on regulatory pluralism theory, we can see that NGO regulation within the UN takes place in a number of ways. Regulatory pluralism understands regulation as not just laws and policies but other processes of control, including self-regulation, and sees 'regulators' not only as state institutions but also as non-state actors, social and economic forces, technologies, and sociological and psychological motivators.[1] Regulation can exert control and as such, part of the purpose of regulation may be to restrict the activities, and ultimately the influence, of NGOs. For example, Jordaan writes that African States tried to minimise the potential impact of NGOs in the Human Rights Council's Universal Periodic Review process when that mechanism was being developed,[2] as discussed further in Chapter 5. It should also be noted that NGOs, even international NGOs, are situated within countries and are subject to regulation within their domestic

---

1 See, e.g. Christine Parker, 'The Pluralization of Regulation' (2008) 9(2) *Theoretical Inquiries in Law* 349.
2 Eduard Jordaan, 'South Africa and the United Nations Human Rights Council' (2014) 36(1) *Human Rights Quarterly* 90.

jurisdiction, often under the auspices of a charities regulator and enjoying tax benefits not available to profit-making entities.[3]

Three main types of regulation are discussed in this chapter – firstly, the formal ECOSOC accreditation process; secondly, association with the UN Department of Global Communications; and thirdly, informal means of regulation that manifest in a variety of ways. The chapter concludes with reflections on what the limitations of the current regulatory regime mean for NGO participation.

2 ECOSOC accreditation

The Economic and Social Council (ECOSOC) is one of the six main organs of the United Nations established by the UN Charter. It is responsible at a policy level for economic, social, and environmental matters, and for the implementation of development goals. In terms of the UN structure, the human rights treaty bodies fall under the remit of ECOSOC but the Human Rights Council does not. Unlike its predecessor, the Commission, the Council reports directly to the General Assembly rather than to ECOSOC. This might imply that NGO ECOSOC accreditation does not apply to the Council; however, Resolution 60/251 provided for NGO participation at the Human Rights Council on the basis of arrangements, including ECOSOC resolution 1996/31.[4] It is notable that ECOSOC was charged with setting up an NGO consultation mechanism as it placed NGOs solely within the economic, social, and environmental sphere and excluded them from matters of peace and security and international relations, overseen by the Security Council and the General Assembly. This situation has improved slightly in the interim years, for example, with the introduction of the Arria Formula meetings of the Security Council and the civil society informal hearings with the General Assembly introduced in 2005.[5] Here, we focus on the regulation of NGO engagement with the UN human rights bodies, rather with the broader UN system.

ECOSOC accreditation has a number of benefits for NGOs. These include the option of attending international conferences and events, making written and oral statements at these events, organising and host 'side events', entering

---

3 See, e.g. Oonagh Breen et al (eds), *Regulatory Waves: Comparative Perspectives on State Regulation and Self-Regulation Policies in the Nonprofit Sector* (Cambridge University Press, 2016).

4 *Human Rights Council*, GA Res 60/251, UN GAOR, 60th sess, Agenda Items 46 and 120, UN Doc A/RES/60/251 (3 April 2006, adopted 15 March 2006) para 11.

5 See, e.g. Jes Martens, *The Future of NGO Participation at the United Nations after the 2005 World Summit* (FES Briefing Paper January 2006, Global Policy Forum).

UN premises and observing open meetings, and having opportunities to network and lobby within these bodies.[6] However, for our purposes it is important to note that ECOSOC accreditation is not required for all NGO engagement with UN human rights bodies. For example, NGOs can make written submissions to UN treaty bodies and the Human Rights Council's Universal Periodic Review (UPR) and can attend informal briefings with treaty bodies and pre-session meetings for the UPR without ECOSOC accreditation.

The current system of ECOSOC accreditation can be traced back to 1945 when Article 71 of the Charter charged ECOSOC with establishing arrangements for consultation:

> The Economic and Social Council may make suitable arrangements for consultation with non-governmental organizations which are concerned with matters within its competence. Such arrangements may be made with international organizations and, where appropriate, with national organizations after consultation with the Member of the United Nations concerned.[7]

In 1946, the General Assembly then established the ECOSOC organ, and moved quickly to recommend ECOSOC adopt arrangements for this consultation.[8] The General Assembly's view, apparently influenced by the trade union movement and others,[9] was that ECOSOC should:

> adopt suitable arrangements enabling the World Federation of Free Trade Unions and the International Co-operative Alliance as well as other international non-governmental organizations whose experience the Economic and Social Council will find necessary to use.[10]

With similar haste, at the first ECOSOC session, the Committee on the Arrangements for Consultation with NGOs was established. The first

---

6 'A Practical Guide to the UN Committee on NGOs' *International Service for Human Rights* (Web Page, July 2017) <www.ishr.ch/news/updated-practical-guide-un-committee-ngos> 5 ('Practical Guide NGOs').

7 *Charter of the United Nations* art 71.

8 *Representation of Non-Governmental Bodies on the Economic and Social Council*, GA Res 4(I), UN GAOR, 1st sess, 33rd plen mtg, UN Doc A/RES/4(I) (14 February 1946) ('*Representation of NGOs ECOSOC*'), quoted in *Yearbook of the United Nations 1946–47* (United Nations, 1947) 551.

9 Anna-Karin Lindblom, *Non-Governmental Organisations in International Law* (Cambridge University Press, 2005) 374.

10 *Representation of NGOs ECOSOC* (n 8).

regulation relating to NGO accreditation was adopted by ECOSOC in July 1946.[11] This resolution established the Committee on Non-Governmental Organizations ('Committee on NGOs') as a standing committee of ECOSOC. The institutional framework established by ECOSOC provided a consultation model for other international organisations, including the Council of Europe and Organization of American States.[12] In 1950, the arrangements were reviewed and ECOSOC Resolution 288(X) was adopted, introducing a requirement that NGOs would undertake to support the work of the UN and promote knowledge of its principles and activities.[13] Today, the Committee on NGOs remains responsible for assessing all applications for NGO accreditation with ECOSOC. The Committee makes recommendations to ECOSOC on the basis of its assessments and in most cases, ECOSOC approves the recommendations.

International NGO the International Service for Human Rights (ISHR) published a 'Practical Guide to the UN Committee on NGOs' to assist NGOs to 'get past the gatekeeper' and obtain consultative status as a means to engage effectively with its human rights system.[14] Certainly the Committee is perceived as a gatekeeper but is also subject to criticism on a number of fronts, including politicised decision-making. This dates back to its early days. For example, Otto reports that in the early 1950s, consultative status was withdrawn from four NGOs as the result of efforts of the United Kingdom and the US, who were unhappy with the NGOs' criticisms of the US and of the UN's role in Korea. The expulsions were achieved despite there being no provision for this in ECOSOC Resolutions.[15]

Government concerns about NGOs' role and influence increased in the following years, in particular the Western domination of NGOs in consultative status, government influence on NGO activities, increasing numbers of NGOs, and NGO criticisms of governments.[16] These led to a review, the outcome of which was the 1968 ECOSOC Resolution 1296 ('Resolution

---

11 *Arrangements for Consultation with Non-governmental Organizations*, ECOSOC Res 3 (13 July 1946).

12 Emanuele Rebasti, 'Beyond Consultative Status: Which Legal Framework for Enhanced Interaction between NGOs and Intergovernmental Organizations?' in Pierre-Marie Dupuy and Luisa Vierucci (eds), *NGOs in International Law: Efficiency in Flexibility?* (Edward Elgar Publishing, 2008) 21, 24.

13 *Review of Consultative Arrangements with Non-Governmental Organizations*, ECOSOC Res 288(X),10th sess, UN Doc E/RES/288(X) (27 February 1950).

14 *Practical Guide NGOs*(n 6).

15 Dianne Otto, 'Nongovernmental Organizations in the United Nations System: The Emerging Role of International Civil Society' (1996) 18(1) *Human Rights Quarterly* 107, 113.

16 Ibid 114.

1296'),[17] which introduced new mechanisms of control, including the option to suspend or withdraw consultative status in certain circumstances, including where there was evidence of secret financial influence by governments or systematic unsubstantiated politically motivated acts by NGOs.[18]

Resolution 1296 redefined criteria for NGOs to gain ECOSOC consultative status, and stated that an NGO 'shall undertake to support the work of the United Nations and to promote knowledge of its principles and activities, in accordance with its own aims and purposes and the nature and scope of its competence and activities'.[19] Other requirements under Resolution 1296 included that the organisation must be broadly representative of its field of competence, have recognised international standing, and cover, where possible, a significant number of countries across various regions of the world; and the proviso that a national organisation would only qualify under exceptional circumstances and then not without the agreement of the relevant UN member State.[20] As Otto noted, controversies around the application of Resolution 1296 included concerns of Western bias, the restrictiveness of the stipulations of cross-regional membership and international standing, effectively excluding national NGOs.[21]

In 1993, ECOSOC established an open-ended working group (OEWG) to update, if necessary, its arrangements for consultation with NGOs and to introduce coherent rules to regulate the participation of NGOs in international UN conferences. As discussed in Chapter 2, there was a significant increase in NGO activity in the early 1990s, including participation in UN World Conferences and the OEWG review came about as a result of pressures from NGOs and was seen to be warranted given large increases in the number of NGOs since Resolution 1296 in 1968. ECOSOC Resolution 1996/31 *Consultative relationship between the United Nations and nongovernmental organizations* was then adopted. It recognised in its preamble 'the need to take into account the full diversity of the non-governmental organizations at the national, regional and international levels'; it provided for a three-level hierarchy of NGO status for accreditation purposes and specified the nature of activity in which each level could engage.[22] The

17 *Arrangements for Consultation with Non-Governmental Organizations*, ESC December 1296 (XLVI), UN ECOSOC Res, 1528th plen mtg, UN Doc E/RES/1296(XLVI) (29 May 1968) ('ECOSOC Res 1296').
18 Otto (n 15) 114.
19 ECOSOC Res 1296 (n 17).
20 Otto (n 15) 107.
21 Ibid 111.
22 *Consultative Relationship between the United Nations and Non-Governmental Organizations*, ECOSOC Res1996/31, 49th plen mtg, UN Doc E/RES/1996/31 (25 July 1996) ('ECOSOC Res 1996/31').

resolution also urged for participation by NGOs from all regions, particularly developing countries.[23]

Whereas engagement with *international* NGOs was the priority as reflected in Article 71 of the UN Charter,[24] due to NGO pressure and a recognition of the important role played by more grassroots NGOs in the early 1990s World Conferences,[25] this changed with Resolution 1996/31, which remains in force today and provides the regulatory framework for formal NGO accreditation with UN human rights bodies. Given the significant changes in the range and scope of NGOs engaging with the UN since the resolution was adopted in 1996, it has been suggested that a revised regulatory regime may be overdue.[26]

The scope of potential NGOs was broadened by Resolution 1996/31 but it was also clear that NGOs' role was to remain limited: 'the arrangements for consultation should not be such as to accord to non-governmental organizations the same rights of participation as are accorded to States'.[27] Rebasti suggests that since any possibility for NGOs to engage in negotiating functions is excluded, NGOs are more like observers than participants;[28] however, he acknowledges that NGOs can influence the agendas of UN human rights bodies. This resonates with the findings discussed in subsequent chapters of this book which also demonstrate that NGOs are in fact active contributors to the work of UN human rights bodies and can influence their recommendations.

Resolution 1996/31 provides that a requirement for ECOSOC status is that the NGO's work must be of 'direct relevance to the aims and purposes of the United Nations',[29] and must be of 'recognised standing within the particular field of its competence'.[30] Additional criteria include being not-for-profit, not advocating violence, and not being a political party or educational institution.[31] NGOs must also have a headquarters, an Executive Officer, transparent decision-making processes, and a constitution.[32] As of

---

23　Ibid para 5.

24　*Charter of the United Nations* art 71.

25　Peter Willetts (ed), '*The Conscience of the World': The Influence of Non Governmental Organisations in the UN System* (David Davies Memorial Institute of International Studies and the Brookings Institution, 1996).

26　Rebasti (n 12) 21.

27　ECOSOC Res 1996/31 (n 22) para 18.

28　Rebasti (n 12) 21, 25.

29　ECOSOC Res 1996/31 (n 22) para 8.

30　Ibid para 9.

31　ECOSOC Res 1296 (n 17) para 17 and ECOSOC Res 1996/31 (n 22) para 25.

32　Ibid paras 10–2. NGOs interested in applying for ECOSOC accreditation can read more about the process at: 'How to Apply for Consultative Status with ECOSOC?' *United*

November 2020, there are 5,728 NGOs listed on the ECOSOC accreditation database.[33]

Under Resolution 1996/31, the highest level of accreditation is 'general consultative status', reserved for large international NGOs who have substantial and sustained contributions to make and are closely involved with the economic and social life of the peoples of the areas they represent.[34] They tend to have broad geographical reach[35]; examples include: Commission of the Churches on International Affairs of the World Council of Churches, and Oxfam International.[36] Therefore, although a wider range of NGOs were included by Resolution 1996/31, a hierarchy was also introduced, with international NGOs at the top.

The second level of accreditation is 'special consultative status'. This is granted to NGOs with special competence, covering selected fields of activity covered by the ECOSOC. These are generally more recent NGOs and smaller in size and scope than those with general status.[37] Examples of NGOs with special consultative status include: Amnesty International, and Arab Red Crescent and Red Cross Organization.[38]

The third level of ECOSOC accreditation is 'roster'. These NGOs are generally narrower in their remit than either general or special status NGOs. NGOs which apply for consultative status but do not fit in any of the other categories are usually included in the Roster and are considered to contribute 'occasional and useful contributions to the work of the Council or its subsidiary bodies'.[39] NGOs can also be placed on the roster due to their consultative status with other UN bodies or specialised agencies, for example, UNESCO or the WHO. Examples of NGOs with roster status include: Asia Pacific Youth Forum, and the World Federation of Public Health Associations.[40]

Nations Department of Economic and Social Affairs (Web Page) <www.un.org/develop ment/desa/dspd/civil-society/ecosoc-status.html>.

33 The database is available at 'Consultative Status with ECOSOC and other accreditations' <https://esango.un.org/civilsociety/displayConsultativeStatusSearch.do?method= redefine> ('ECOSOC Database').

34 ECOSOC Res 1996/31 (n 22) para 22.

35 'Introduction to ECOSOC Consultative Status'*NGO Branch: Department of Economic and Social Affairs* (Web Page) <http://csonet.org/index.php?menu=30>.

36 United Nations Economic and Social Council, *List of Non-Governmental Organizations in Consultative Status with the Economic and Social Council as of 1 September 2014*, UN Doc E/2014/INF/5 <http://csonet.org/content/documents/E-2014-INF-5%20Issued.pdf>.

37 ECOSOC Res 1996/31 (n 22) para 22.

38 ECOSOC Database (n 33).

39 Introduction to ECOSOC Consultative Status (n 35).

40 ECOSOC Database (n 33).

As a result of Resolution 1996/31, membership of the Committee on NGOs is based on equitable geographical distribution, responding to criticisms of Western bias.[41] The Committee comprises 19 members – five from African states, four from Asian states, two from Eastern European states, four from Latin American and Caribbean states, and four from the Western European and others groups (WEOG).[42] Today, the criticisms of the Committee on NGOs endure. A robust analysis of decisions by the NGO committee from 2005 to 2015 by Vromen concludes that the broad, vague criteria in Resolution 1996/31, together with Article 15 of the resolution, which states that interpreting the norms is the prerogative of the Council and the Committee, leaves the Committee with broad discretion in interpreting the resolution.[43] She notes that broad interpretation of the criteria causes a lot of debate among the Committee members – in most cases in fact, and almost all refusals of accreditation are not made with consensus. She also notes that grounds for the Committee's decisions are hard to trace back to the criteria in Resolution 1996/31, particularly decisions made regarding NGOs advocating for LGBTI rights.[44] According to a 2020 UN report on civil society space, NGOs and civil society organisations with or without consultative status with ECOSOC continue to face multiple barriers to participation at UN fora and the rules of the Committee on NGOs are often described as a hurdle to civil society participation in the UN.[45]

3 Association with the Department of Global Communities (DGC)

A less formal association with UN bodies is available via the Department of Global Communications (formerly the Department of Public Information). Some NGOs may also have ECOSOC status as ECOSOC and the DGC operate two separate systems. There are more NGOs accredited with ECOSOC than associated with DGC. NGOs recognised by the DGC tend to

41   Otto (n 15) 107, 115.
42   Rosa Freedman and Ruth Houghton, 'Two Steps Forward, One Step Back: Politicisation of the Human Rights Council' (2017) 17(4) *Human Rights Law Review* 753.
43   Simone Vromen, 'The Council Committee on NGOs: An Analysis of the Reports of the Council Committee on NGOs between 2005 and 2015' (2017) 13(1) *Utrecht Law Review* 82.
44   Ibid.
45   Human Rights Council, *Annual Report of the United Nations High Commissioner for Human Rights and Reports of the Office of the High Commissioner and the Secretary-General*, 44th sess, Agenda Items 2 and 3, UN Doc A/HRC/44/25 (20 April 2020) para 24.

have fewer privileges to participate in UN intergovernmental meetings. The DGC is a less formal and rigid way of engaging with NGOs, but is more focused on mutual information sharing than ECOSOC.

Benefits of DGC association include increasing the NGO's profile by having it listed in the public directory, allowing participation in the UN Civil Society Conference and briefings, and accessing UN civil society resources in New York.[46] Criteria for association include supporting the principles of the UN Charter, being a 'reputable civil society organization', and being operational as a not-for-profit for at least 2 years.[47]

In 2004, the Cardoso Report recommended that all UN accreditation processes be simplified, and amalgamated into a single mechanism under the authority of the General Assembly. It was also recommended that the General Assembly should regularly invite contributions to its committees and special sessions by organisations offering high-quality independent input.[48]

The amalgamation of accreditation processes did not take place but the General Assembly did instigate informal briefings with NGOs in 2005.

4 Other forms of NGO regulation at the UN

As signposted in the chapter introduction, regulation can be both formal and informal. The preceding sections have discussed the formal regulation of NGOs in UN human rights bodies but there are also informal modes of regulation at play.

One example is that in my research, some interviewees indicated that suspect NGO information is 'filtered out' by the OHCHR secretariat before it gets to treaty bodies. They can exclude NGO reports to any treaty body if they are:

> unsubstantiated in any way ... what's obviously inflammatory or polit-
> ically motivated. We discount this type of information before it gets
> to the treaty body to prevent too much paperwork which would eat up
> time. If it's manifestly one-sided.[49]

---

46 'Formal Association with the Department of Global Communications' *United Nations Civil Society Unit* (Web Page) <https://outreach.un.org/ngorelations/content/association>.
47 Ibid.
48 *We the Peoples: Civil Society, the United Nations and Global Governance: Report of the Panel of Eminent Persons on United Nations – Civil Society Relations*, UN GAOR, 58th sess, Agenda Item 59, UN Doc A/58/817 (11 June 2004) 16.
49 Office of the High Commissioner for Human Rights interviewee, interview conducted 28 April 2015, Geneva.

Treaty body members interviewed seemed unaware of the behind-the-scenes filtering by the OHCHR but applied their own filter to NGO information they deemed to be lacking credibility.[50] This included NGOs whose position appeared to contradict the object and purpose of the relevant treaty, or NGOs that 'were more supportive of the government than the government themselves were',[51] i.e. GONGOs. Some also described filtering out information or recommendations they saw as inaccurate or problematic, based on their knowledge and expertise.[52]

These findings resonate with Billaud's ethnographic study of the Human Rights Council which exposed that there are criteria for the selection of NGO submissions for inclusion in the UPR 'stakeholder summary' report.[53] These criteria are not made public for NGOs and are constantly negotiated and re-interpreted by those drafting the stakeholder summary reports.[54] For example, priority may in fact be given to NGOs with ECOSOC accreditation, even though this is not required to submit a report. Also, NGO contributions may be excluded if they contain 'second-hand information' or were written in a non-official UN language.[55] These constraints ignore the reality of resource-poor NGOs, particularly from the Global South, who may have valid issues to raise but may not have the resources to present them effectively according to these unwritten rules. The covert rules and politicised nature of the UPR also mean that reports by GONGOs could be included in the stakeholder summary report.[56] For example, in Venezuela's UPR, where 80 per cent of 'civil society' contributions came from Communal Councils praising Government policies, the Secretariat chose not to dismiss these but rather grouped them together so they could be referred to collectively in the stakeholder summary report.[57]

In addition to the informal 'filtering' carried out by the OHCHR secretariat, another type of informal regulation is performed by NGOs. In Chapter 1, I discussed the 'gatekeeper NGO'. These NGOs, typically

---

50 Treaty body independent expert, interview conducted 28 April 2015, Geneva.

51 Treaty body independent expert, interview conducted 30 April 2015, Geneva.

52 Ibid.

53 Julie Billaud, 'Keepers of the Truth: Producing "Transparent" Documents for the Universal Periodic Review' in Hilary Charlesworth and Emma Larking (eds), *Human Rights and the Universal Periodic Review: Rituals and Ritualism* (Cambridge University Press, 2015) 70.

54 Ibid.

55 Ibid.

56 For a brief discussion of GONGOs, see Kerstin Martens, 'Examining the (Non-)Status of NGOs in International Law' (2003) 10(2) *Indiana Journal of Global Legal Studies* 1, 8.

57 Billaud (n 53) 68.

international in nature, can act as gatekeepers by being prescriptive about access to UN human rights bodies or related meetings, by controlling access and potentially preventing access to them. Examples include UPR-Info which acts as gatekeeper NGO for its own pre-sessions where NGOs and other civil society actors are brought together with representatives from States' Permanent Missions to present on the human rights situation of States prior to their UPR. UPR-Info takes expressions of interests for speaking slots at these pre-sessions and manages the format, duration, and logistics of the sessions.[58] The pre-sessions and UPR-Info's management of the associated logistics were seen as useful by government representatives, for example: 'The pre-sessions are extremely useful because they come simultaneously and it gives you ample opportunity to verify information, even with the State under review on a bilateral basis and to prepare well in advance'.[59] Another example is International Women's Rights Action Watch (IWRAW) which interviewees reported as having a gatekeeper role for the Committee on the Elimination of Discrimination Against Women (CEDAW). Gatekeepers, whether NGOs or UN bodies, arise out of a perceived need. As noted in the previous chapter, there has been an exponential growth in the number of NGOs over the past 70 years, many of them are seeking to engage with the UN system, and there is a practical need to manage this engagement. In interviews, OHCHR staff, treaty body members, and to a lesser extent, Government interviewees, consistently referred to the deluge of information they receive from NGOs, which is impossible for them to read. Therefore, informal gatekeepers tend to be more effective at managing *quantity* but are less equipped to manage *quality*, which requires a more robust regulatory approach.

5 Discussion

ECOSOC accreditation remains the only formal accreditation for NGOs engaging with UN human rights bodies. Those not requiring (or not being granted) accreditation with ECOSOC have the option of association with the DGC – or NGOs may hold both DGC association and ECOSOC accreditation. Accreditation brings benefits to NGOs in terms of options for participation and, as a regulatory system, it offers some level of legitimacy and transparency to UN engagement with NGOs. The system has been

---

58 Roland Chauville, UPR-Info, interview conducted Geneva (28 April 2017).
59 Government representative, member of Human Rights Council, interview conducted 11 November 2015, Geneva.

refined over the years but in its basic form, it has existed since 1946 and has informed the development of similar models for consultation in other international organisations.

Nonetheless, ECOSOC accreditation has a number of challenges. Firstly, the accreditation process and in particular the decision-making of the Committee on NGOs has been subject to harsh criticism for many years.[60] Secondly, ECOSOC accreditation is not required for all NGO engagement with UN human rights bodies, such as briefing treaty bodies or submitting reports to the UPR. This causes further potential problems. One issue is that in the absence of a formal regulatory regime, informal systems of regulation arise. These include gatekeeping by the OHCHR in its secretariat role and by NGOs. However, interviews with the OHCHR and treaty bodies indicates that the absence of formal regulation for engagement with these mechanisms means that State representatives on the Human Rights Council and independent experts on the treaty bodies are often overwhelmed with information from NGOs. In this scenario, it is understandable that informal regulation occurs. A concern though is that for some NGOs, it could present an additional barrier to accessing the UN.

A final issue is that UN bodies may be subject to advances from questionable actors, such as GONGOs or servile NGOs. An ineffective regulatory regime that allows these actors – whose agendas may not align with the promotion and protection of international human rights law – risks politicising the agendas of UN human rights bodies, undermining the integrity of NGOs in general and co-opting civil society space at the UN. Conversely, more widespread, stricter, or more onerous regulation of NGO engagement with UN human rights bodies might inadvertently dissuade genuine NGOs from applying for accreditation. Allowing a range of civil society actors to submit reports to the Human Rights Council's UPR, or to brief a human rights treaty body, ensures these bodies are accessible and that they hear concerns from people 'on the ground', and not just from those more established NGOs with ECOSOC status.

6   Conclusion

The foundation for the NGO role in the UN, and for the regulation of NGO engagement, lies in Article 71 of the Charter which provided for 'consultation' with ECOSOC. A system of accreditation was developed and refined

---

60   Otto (n 15); see, e.g. 'UN Committee on NGOs: Don't Deny NGO the Right to Speak' *International Service for Human Rights* (Web Page, 29 January 2016) <www.ishr.ch/news/un-committee-ngos-dont-deny-ngo-right-speak>.

from 1946 onwards, with the most recent resolution of 1996/31 remaining in force today. This enables NGOs to apply for ECOSOC accreditation. Their applications are assessed by the Committee on NGOs – a body which has been subject to criticism almost since its inception. There are three tiers of ECOSOC accreditation, each with a different level of privileges in terms of participation in UN bodies: general consultative status, special consultative status, and roster. There is also the option to seek association with the UN's Department of Global Communities (DGC). Despite these formal systems of regulation, neither ECOSOC nor DGC accreditation is required for all NGO engagement with UN human rights bodies. Drawing on regulatory pluralism theory, there is evidence of other, informal regulatory regimes at work, some elements of which can be problematic by creating barriers to accessing UN bodies, or conversely may present opportunities for questionable actors, such as GONGOs, to engage with UN bodies. An effective system of regulation that screens for such actors, while avoiding undue regulatory burdens, or barriers to access, for (often under-funded) NGOs, remains elusive.

4   NGOs, treaties, and treaty bodies

1 Introduction

There are nine core UN human rights treaties, introduced to give legal effect to the non-binding provisions of the UDHR and to introduce new rights and protect specific groups.[1] As such, these treaties form the cornerstone of international human rights law as they contain the legally binding human rights obligations for States parties. Each of the UN's nine core human rights treaties has its own Committee to monitor implementation of the treaty among States parties, primarily through considering periodic reports.[2] Much of the existing research on the NGO role in international

---

1 The nine core treaties are, ordered by date of adoption by the General Assembly: *International Convention on the Elimination of All Forms of Racial Discrimination*, opened for signature 21 December 1965, 660 UNTS 195 (entered into force 4 January 1969) ('ICERD'); *International Covenant on Civil and Political Rights*, opened for signature 16 December 1966, 999 UNTS 171 (entered into force 23 March 1976) ('ICCPR'); *International Covenant on Economic, Social and Cultural Rights,* opened for signature 16 December 1966, 993 UNTS 3 (entered into force 3 January 1976) ('ICESCR'); *Convention on the Elimination of All Forms of Discrimination against Women,* opened for signature 1 March 1980, 1249 UNTS 13 (entered into force 3 September 1981) ('CEDAW'); *International Convention against Torture and Other Cruel, Inhuman and Degrading Treatment or Punishment,* opened for signature 10 December 1984, 1465 UNTS 85 (entered into force 26 June 1987) ('CAT'); *Convention on the Rights of the Child,* opened for signature 20 November 1989, 1577 UNTS 3 (entered into force 2 September 1990) ('CRoC'); *International Convention on the Protection of the Rights of All Migrant Workers and Members of their Families,* opened for signature 18 December 1990, 2220 UNTS 3 (entered into force 1 July 2003); *International Convention for the Protection of All Persons from Enforced Disappearance,* opened for signature 20 December 2006, 2716 UNTS 3 (entered into force 23 December 2010); *Convention on the Rights of Persons with Disabilities,* opened for signature 13 Dec 2006, 2515 UNTS 3 (entered into force 3 May 2008).
2 The terms UN Committee and treaty body are both used in this chapter, with the same meaning.

human rights law focuses on the NGO role in engaging with UN treaty bodies. This is unsurprising, as the treaty bodies were the testing ground for NGO engagement in human rights advocacy at the UN and are the longest standing fora of engagement, as discussed in Chapter 2.

The NGO influence with regard to UN human rights treaties can be felt from the drafting stage through to the implementation, monitoring, and interpretation of treaties. This chapter begins by discussing NGOs' active involvement in the drafting of the UN human rights treaties – particularly the later treaties – and in other instruments and interpretive texts. This is followed by an analysis of the NGO role and influence in the State-reporting mechanism of the treaty bodies, and finally, the NGO role in the treaty body individual complaint process. It concludes that NGOs play a critical role in providing local and international expertise and governance through the drafting of treaties, support for strategic litigation on significant rights issues through the individual complaints process, and provision of critical information and suitable recommendations in State reporting.

2 NGOs and the drafting of treaties

In addition to the NGO influence on the drafting of the UN Charter as discussed in Chapter 2, Charnovitz notes that most NGO activity at the UN from 1950 to 1971 was in the area of human rights, with 30 NGOs taking part in the conference that drafted the Convention on Refugees in the early 1950s, for example.[3] He notes that NGOs were also influential in drafting the International Covenant on Civil and Political Rights ('ICCPR') and the International Covenant on Economic, Social and Cultural Rights ('ICE-SCR'), discussed in Chapter 2, and played a particularly significant role in the drafting of the *UN Convention on the Rights of the Child* ('CRoC').[4]

Cohen charts the development of CRoC and traces its roots to NGO 'Save the Children International Union' ('SCIU'). SCIU drafted the first declaration of the rights of the child in 1924, which was adopted by the League of Nations and inspired the 1959 UN Declaration of the Rights of the Child.[5] 1979 was designated as the International Year of the Child by the UN and the General Assembly authorised the Commission on Human Rights to draft a convention on children's rights. A Working Group was

---

3 Steve Charnovitz, 'Two Centuries of Participation: NGOs and International Governance' (1997) 18(2) *Michigan Journal of International Law* 183, 258.

4 Ibid.

5 Cynthia Price Cohen, 'The Role of Nongovernmental Organizations in the Drafting of the Convention on the Rights of the Child' (1990) 12(1) *Human Rights Quarterly* 137, 138.

established by the Commission and NGOs were active participants from the beginning, not only as observers but through written and oral interventions.[6] Cohen identified successful features and activities of the NGO group (which became known as the 'Informal NGO Ad Hoc Group on the Drafting of the Convention on the Rights of the Child'), including their coordinated approach, producing reports, proposing or amending text of articles for the drafting process, and lobbying governments.

Lindkvist explains that the Swedish Save the Children Federation ('Rädda Barnen') played a very significant role in facilitating NGO cooperation and shaping the drafting group discussions.[7] She identifies a crucial turning point for the organisation and its influence in 1981 when it was granted ECOSOC accreditation – a remarkable achievement given that the consultative status was reserved for international NGOs, transforming it from a domestic to an international NGO.[8] Van Boven also acknowledges the leadership role played by NGO 'Defence for Children International' in the Informal NGO Ad Hoc Group.[9] Overall, NGO influence on the drafting of the CRoC was as a result of many NGOs acting through the Informal NGO Ad Hoc Group (which had 35 members), or acting solo.[10]

Although government delegates were initially suspicious of NGO participation, this changed over six years of drafting and when the Convention was adopted by the Commission on Human Rights, nearly every government statement in support of the Convention made complimentary references to the important role of NGOs in the drafting process.[11] Cohen reflected: 'When one looks at the completed draft of the Convention on the Rights of the Child, the imprint of the NGO Group can be found in almost every article'.[12] It is not surprising then that the final Convention then contains Article 45 (a), which provides that the CRoC Committee 'may invite . . . other competent bodies as it may consider appropriate to provide expert advice on the implementation of the Convention in areas falling within the scope of their respective mandates'. The Committee's rules confirm that

---

6 Ibid 139.
7 Linde Lindkvist, 'Rights for the World's Children: Rädda Barnen and the Making of the UN Convention on the Rights of the Child' (2018) 36(3) *Nordic Journal of Human Rights* 287.
8 Ibid 295.
9 Theo van Boven, 'The Role of Non-Governmental Organizations in International Human Rights Standard-Setting: A Prerequisite of Democracy' (1990) 20(2) *California Western International Law Journal* 207, 215.
10 Ibid.
11 Cohen (n 5) 145.
12 Ibid 142.

'other competent bodies' include NGOs.[13] However, not all of the NGO Group's initiatives were successful, such as the failure to raise the minimum age for participation in armed combat to 18 from the 15-year-old minimum contained in the Geneva Protocols.[14]

The progress made by NGOs engaged with the drafting of the CRoC provided an important precedent when it came to the drafting of the UN Convention on the Rights of Persons with Disabilities ('CRPD'). In the lead-up to the CRPD, there were many years of activism whereby NGOs and others mobilised the international community to take disability rights seriously, particularly during the drafting of the CRPD.[15] Sabatello and Schulze argue that:

> civil society participation in the process exceeded by far previous cases of involvement in the formulation of international human rights treaties. It has, in fact, taken the idea of 'new diplomacy,' referring to civil society's involvement in international processes, to a new level.[16]

From the beginning, NGO engagement in drafting was more formalised than it had been in previous treaties. The General Assembly adopted a resolution in December 2001 to establish an Ad Hoc Committee to consider drafting a disability rights convention and invited NGOs, along with States and other relevant bodies, to make contributions.[17] The resolution permitted NGOs to make contributions 'based on the practice of the UN', but if this was a reference to ECOSOC accreditation, many disability rights NGOs were not accredited. Following lobbying by NGOs, two important resolutions were adopted that included provisions for a separate accreditation process for groups who lacked accreditation. By the seventh session, 110 disability organisations were accredited to participate in the sessions and almost 500 individuals, mostly persons with disabilities, attended the final round of negotiations.[18] The resolutions also allowed accredited NGOs to attend any public meeting of the Committee and this was later extended to informal consultations and closed meetings, to intervene in the plenary,

13 CRoC, *Provisional Rules of Procedure*, UN Doc CRC/C/4 (14 November 1991).
14 Cohen (n 5) 143.
15 Maya Sabatello and Marianne Schulze (eds), *Human Rights and Disability Advocacy* (University of Pennsylvania Press, 2014) 5.
16 Ibid.
17 Ibid 6.
18 Ibid.

to receive copies of official documents, and to make written or other presentations.[19] This reflects effective lobbying for the disability movement's mantra of 'nothing about us without us'. This approach is also credited with influencing more recent UN instruments, such as the Sustainable Development Goals (SDGs), which, unlike the Millennium Development Goals, make express provision for people with disabilities.[20] In the drafting of the CRPD, NGO effectiveness could be as a result of many factors, including more openness to civil society in global governance, but some key factors might be effective coalitions and networks, expert contributions – including lived experience – and effective use of technology.[21]

NGOs have also contributed to the drafting of treaty body general comments or general recommendations. General comments or general recommendations (depending on the treaty) serve to interpret the treaty, to clarify the scope and meaning of the provisions and States parties' obligations.[22] For example, for the Human Rights Committee, these are based on Article 40 (4) of the ICCPR, which provides that the Committee may transmit 'such general comments as it may consider appropriate' to all States parties.[23] An example of NGO contribution to this process is provided by Gaer who describes how the NGO 'International League for Human Rights' helped the Committee on the Elimination of Discrimination against Women (CEDAW) formulate what later became the milestone general recommendation on violence against women (General Recommendation 19).[24] The International League for Human Rights' strategy was to hold a conference focusing on violence against women just prior to the opening of the CEDAW session in January 1992, with NGO the International Women's Rights Action Watch, attended by NGOs, academics, and members of CEDAW. The key purpose of the conference was 'to help the CEDAW . . . members draft a weightier and more legally oriented general recommendation on violence by providing them with the detailed legal documentation prepared for the conference'.[25] The report they prepared served as the draft for what became

19 Ibid.
20 Elizabeth Lockwood, ' "Nothing About Us Without Us": Disability, the SDGs and the UNCRPD', *Future Learn* <www.futurelearn.com/courses/global-disability/0/steps/37575>.
21 Maya Sabatello, 'The New Diplomacy' in Sabatello and Schulze (eds) (n 13) 239.
22 Office of the High Commissioner for Human Rights, *Civil and Political Rights: The Human Rights Committee*, Fact Sheet No. 15 (Rev.1) (May 2005) <www.ohchr.org/Documents/Publications/FactSheet15rev.1en.pdf>.
23 ICCPR (n 1), Article 40 (4).
24 Felice D Gaer, 'Implementing International Human Rights Norms: UN Human Rights Treaty Bodies and NGOs' (2003) 2(3) *Journal of Human Rights* 339, 347–8.
25 Ibid.

General Recommendation 19 and served as a model for the drafting of further CEDAW general recommendations.[26]

Beyond the core UN human rights treaties, there is significant evidence of the influence of NGOs in the drafting of international human rights instruments and in pressuring governments to sign and ratify them. For example, Gallagher and Ngozi note that drafting of the Trafficking Protocol was supported by international and regional bodies, mainstream human rights organisations, and new anti-trafficking NGOs.[27] Augustínyová and Dumbryte discuss the significance of NGOs in the drafting of the Rome Statute of the International Criminal Court.[28] In this case, NGOs formed 'the Coalition for the ICC' and actively engaged State representatives during the Rome Conference, influencing the provisions of the final Statute, including the Prosecutor's power to initiate investigations and the prohibition of a wide range of sexual and gender-based crimes.[29] This legacy is reflected in Article 44 (4) of the Rome Statute which provides that:

> The Court may, in exceptional circumstances, employ the expertise of gratis personnel offered by States Parties, intergovernmental organizations, or non-governmental organizations to assist with the work of any of the organs of the Court.[30]

In another well-known example, Chandhoke discusses the victory of global NGOs' campaign pressurising governments to draft a treaty to ban the production, the stockpiling, and the export of landmines.[31] Almost 1,000 transnational NGOs coordinated the campaign on the treaty to ban landmines. It was signed in 1997 and the International Campaign to Ban Landmines and

---

26 Ibid.

27 Anne T Gallagher and Joy Ngozi Ezeilo, 'The UN Special Rapporteur on Trafficking: A Turbulent Decade in Review' (2015) 37(4) *Human Rights Quarterly* 913, 916.

28 Gabriela Augustínyová and Aiste Dumbryte, 'The Indispensable Role of Non-Governmental Organizations in the Creation and Functioning of the International Criminal Court' in Alexander J Bělohlávek, Naděžda Rozehnalová and Filip Černý (eds), *Czech Yearbook of International Law – The Role of Governmental and Non-Governmental Organizations in the 21st Century* (Juris Publishing, 2014) 39.

29 Ibid.

30 *Rome Statute of the International Criminal Court*, opened for signature 17 July 1998, 2187 UNTS 3 (entered into force 1 July 2002).

31 Neera Chandhoke, 'The Limits of Global Civil Society' in Helmut K Anheier, Marlies Glasius and Mary Kaldor (eds), *Global Civil Society* (Oxford University Press, 2002) 35, 38–9.

its representative, Jody Williams, were awarded the Nobel Peace Prize.[32] The citation at the award-giving ceremony spoke of their unique effort that made it possible to express and mediate a broad wave of popular commitment in an unprecedented way.

3 NGOs and treaty body State reporting[33]

Treaty body State reporting is the key monitoring mechanism for States' compliance with their treaty obligations. Each treaty specifies a reporting frequency, usually every few years. For example, Article 19 (1) of the Convention against Torture and Other Cruel, Inhuman or Degrading Treatment or Punishment provides that States parties shall submit their first report within one year of the entry into force of the Convention for that State party and every four years thereafter.[34] However, in reality the treaty bodies experience significant backlogs, States often report late (if at all in some cases), and treaty bodies often request reports to combine two reporting periods.[35] As such the reporting deadlines are somewhat meaningless. Nonetheless, significant work continues in development of a list of key topics for each State review (the 'List of Issues Prior to Reporting' or 'LOIPR'), then the submission of reports from States, analysis of these by the treaty body, discussion between the State and treaty body in a 'constructive dialogue' at Palais Wilson in Geneva, the publication of comments and recommendations to the State in 'concluding observations', and the 'follow-up' procedure. NGOs can be involved at each of these stages. They can influence the selection of the LOIPR, provide shadow or alternative reports to supplement or critique information provided by States, brief Committee members to influence the questions asked during the constructive dialogue and the recommendations made in 'concluding observations', and inform implementation through 'follow-up' and in the next reporting cycle.

---

32 Ibid.

33 Some of the content in this section has been adapted from: Fiona McGaughey, 'The "Curious Grapevine": 70 Years of Non-Governmental Organisations in the United Nations Human Rights System' in Noelle Higgins et al (eds), *The Universal Declaration of Human Rights at Seventy: A Review of Successes and Challenges* (Clarus Press Ltd, 2020) ('Curious Grapevine').

34 CAT (n 1) art 19(1).

35 For more analysis of these issues, see the body of literature on treaty body reform/strengthening, including: United Nations General Assembly, *Strengthening and Enhancing the Effective Functioning of the Human Rights Treaty Body System*, GA Res 68/268, UN GAOR, 68th sess, Agenda Item 125, UN Doc A/RES/68/268 (9 April 2014); Michael O'Flaherty, 'Reform of the UN Human Rights Treaty Body System: Locating the Dublin Statement' (2010) 10(2) *Human Rights Law Review* 319.

As discussed in Chapter 2, these opportunities for NGOs were carved out by NGOs despite the lack of provision for a formal role for them, as they saw the opportunity to raise concerns about States' compliance with their treaty obligations. In Chapter 3, the regulation of NGO engagement through ECOSOC was discussed but it is important to note that for much of the engagement with treaty bodies, ECOSOC accreditation has never been required for NGOs to submit a report or to brief the Committees.[36] Today, all Committees engage with NGOs in broadly similar ways, as such, this section provides an overview and analysis of the most common means of engagement and influence with treaty bodies. The Chairs of the Committees co-operate with each other and the UN is working towards more simplified reporting with common working methods among the Committees.[37] However, it is important to note that there are some minor variations across the treaty bodies, such as the role for NGOs and others in Article 45 (a) of the *Convention on the Rights of the Child*, which provides that the Committee 'may invite . . . other competent bodies as it may consider appropriate to provide expert advice on the implementation of the Convention in areas falling within the scope of their respective mandates'.[38]

NGO reports may be submitted to the Committees by individual NGOs or by coalitions of NGOs. An NGO coalition report can be mutually beneficial to the UN Committee and to NGOs – the endorsement of multiple, sometimes even hundreds, of NGOs brings added legitimacy. For resource-poor NGOs, being part of a coalition is more cost-effective. A disadvantage is that their human rights issues of concern may get lost in the larger report. NGO reports are an informal part of the process and as such there are no formal restrictions on word limit, nor do the OHCHR Secretariats generally translate NGO reports into the working languages of the Committees.[39] The lack of a word limit is problematic, as in my interviews with Committee members, some expressed being inundated by NGO reports, some of which are 'very long'; for example, a Committee member interviewee commented:

The very first State in the very first week was Canada and there was a pile of submissions two feet high and many of them very duplicative

---

36 International Service for Human Rights, *Simple Guide to Treaty Bodies* (2015) 38 ('*Guide to Treaty Bodies*'); Daisuke Shirane, *ICERD and CERD: A Guide for Civil Society Actors* (The International Movement Against All Forms of Discrimination and Racism, 2011) <www.ohchr.org/Documents/HRBodies/CERD/ICERDManual.pdf>.

37 Navanetham Pillay, *Strengthening the United Nations Human Rights Treaty Body System: A Report by the United Nations High Commissioner for Human Rights* (Office of the High Commissioner for Human Rights, June 2012).

38 CRoC (n 1).

39 See, e.g. UN Committee on the Elimination of Racial Discrimination, *NGO Information Note*, 84th sess (3 to 21 February 2014).

so it's impossible, even if a Committee member wanted to go through them all, to do so.[40]

Some Committee members attend informal NGO briefing sessions related to each State under review, often held at lunchtime, where NGOs present their concerns to the Committee members. Some Committees rely heavily on a key NGO – a gatekeeper to some extent – to manage their engagement with NGOs.[41] For example, the Centre for Civil and Political Rights facilitates engagement with the Human Rights Committee.

My observation confirmed that lunchtime briefings were not always well attended by Committee members.[42] These short, one-hour meetings, held in a standard meeting room, without official interpreting, do not compare favourably with the formal, lengthy constructive dialogue held in conference rooms decked with interpreters behind glass partitions. It is clear that States parties are the primary actors and that NGOs remain soundly on a lesser and more informal footing. NGOs also meet informally with Committee members on an *ad hoc* basis, and it was this author's observation that the cafeteria at Palais Wilson was a hive of NGO activity, where there were ongoing meetings between Committee members and NGO representatives. One Committee member interviewee recommended that NGOs 'make it your business to talk to people on the Committee'.[43] Some Committees have a 'country rapporteur' who leads the review for a specific State and they can be particularly useful for NGOs to engage with, one commented:

> there are less formal meetings over lunch or you can meet as individual committee members with them in the cafeteria just to have coffee or something. I will try to do that if I'm the rapporteur, I'll try to meet with them in addition to the settings that are available to all the committee members. Then in those meetings I try to assess their views about the significance of the problems.[44]

There has been some progress with the use of technology, such as video-conferencing for NGO briefings or individual meetings,[45] but this is by no

---

40 Committee Member Interviewee, interview conducted 28 April 2015, Geneva.

41 Fiona McGaughey, 'From Gatekeepers to GONGOs: A Taxonomy of Non-Governmental Organisations Engaging with United Nations Human Rights Mechanisms' (2018) 36(2) *Netherlands Quarterly of Human Rights* 111 ('From Gatekeepers to GONGOs').

42 Curious Grapevine (n 33).

43 Committee Member Interviewee, interview conducted 29 April 2015, Geneva.

44 Committee Member Interviewee, interview conducted 28 April 2015, Geneva.

45 *Guide to Treaty Bodies* (n 36) 42.

means widespread and well established across the treaty bodies. It is an area of significant potential as the cost and logistical challenges of travelling to Geneva make the treaty bodies inaccessible for many NGOs in the Global South and elsewhere. It remains to be seen whether altered working arrangements during the COVID-19 pandemic, whereby some of the work of UN bodies was carried out remotely, will continue in subsequent years. In addition to NGO briefings, some Committees have other means of engaging with NGOs. For example, since 2012, all CERD Committee members attend a weekly NGO briefing with NGOs from all States being reviewed in a given week.[46] Additional pressure to engage in a more structured way with NGOs came from the treaty body reform agenda,[47] and a meeting with NGO representatives at the Committee's 77th session, on 3 August 2010, where strengthening cooperation with NGOs was discussed.[48] As a result, weekly briefings were introduced, in which NGOs from all States under review can participate.

NGO briefings are generally held outside of the formal review with governments. The meeting with the State under review, called the constructive dialogue, is held in public plenary sessions and generally spread across two half-day sessions lasting several hours in total. NGOs generally have no speaking rights at these sessions but can attend as observers.[49] In State reporting to UN Committees, the constructive dialogue has been described as 'the centrepiece of the exercise'.[50] It tends to take the form of diplomatic pleasantries on both sides, positive comments on progress and questions on areas of concern arising from the State's report from the Committee, and responses from the government. Despite the diplomacy, a government interviewee described treaty body constructive dialogues as 'like an inquisition'.[51] Constructive dialogues between Committees and States parties can now be viewed online.[52] The questions asked of States parties may be informed by NGO reports,[53] or informal briefings.

---

46 United Nations General Assembly, *Report of the Committee on the Elimination of Racial Discrimination*, UN GAOR, 67thsess, Supp No 18, UN Doc A/67/18 (13 February – 9 March 2012) para 65 ('*CERD Report 2012*').

47 Curious Grapevine (n 33).

48 *CERD Report 2012* (n 44) para 65.

49 For additional information on the constructive dialogue, see Michael O'Flaherty, *The UN and Human Rights: Practice Before the Treaty Bodies* (Martinus Nijhoff Publishers, 2002) ch 1.

50 Nigel S Rodley, 'UN Treaty Bodies and the Human Rights Council' in Helen Keller and Geir Ulfstein (eds), *UN Human Rights Treaty Bodies: Law and Legitimacy* (Cambridge University Press, 2012) 336.

51 Curious Grapevine (n 33).

52 *UN Treaty Body Webcast* <www.treatybodywebcast.org/category/webcast-archives/>

53 David P Forsythe, *Human Rights in International Relations* (Cambridge University Press, 2006) 203–4.

The importance of the NGO role in treaty body monitoring is primarily the provision of critical, 'on the ground' information, offering a practical, cost-effective solution to fill a gap in the UN system. Leading human rights scholars have claimed that in their role of providing alternative information to UN Committees, NGOs play a significant role in State reporting.[54] The importance of information provided by NGOs has also been acknowledged by the UN Secretary General,[55] by Committee members in interviews for this study, and by expert scholars.[56] Thornberry and Cushman both argue that there is a lack of resources available to the OHCHR staff and Committee members to undertake fact-finding on the human rights situation in each State.[57] This was also a recurrent theme in my interviews, as one of the OHCHR staff members interviewed stated: 'People forget that the treaty body system does not have a fact finding tool of its own, unlike Special Rapporteurs who move, who go and research and make reports but independent experts sit in Geneva'.[58] Furthermore, government reports are unlikely to highlight their own shortcomings, tending rather to be 'descriptive, formalistic, legalistic and self-congratulatory, rather than reflective and focused on substance and practical realities, and problems encountered'.[59] The gap for UN Committees includes this content on practical realities and problems; a gap filled by reports from civil society actors, predominantly NGOs.

In my interviews, OHCHR staff and treaty body members perceived NGOs to play an important role in State reporting; using words, such as 'important', 'very important', and 'very useful'. One used much more emphatic language, such as 'critical'; and 'absolutely crucial'.[60] The provision of critical information was particularly valued and most people I interviewed perceived the NGO role as a balance in the State-reporting system,

---

54 See, e.g. Laurie S Wiseberg, 'The Role of Non-Governmental Organizations (NGOs) in the Protection and Enforcement of Human Rights' in Janusz Symonides (ed), *Human Rights: International Protection, Monitoring, Enforcement* (UNESCO Publishing, 2003) 347 ('Role of NGOs in Protection of Human Rights'); Michael Freeman, *Human Rights: An Interdisciplinary Approach* (Polity Press, 2nd ed, 2011) 152.

55 General Assembly 11 June 2004 *Fifty-eighth session Agenda item 59 Strengthening of the United Nations system*, UN Doc A/58/817.

56 Patrick Thornberry, 'Confronting Racial Discrimination: A CERD Perspective' (2005) 5(2) *Human Rights Law Review* 239, 249.

57 Ibid; Thomas Cushman (ed), *Handbook of Human Rights* (Routledge, 2012) 350.

58 Curious Grapevine (n 33).

59 Christof H Heyns and Frans Viljoen, *The Impact of the United Nations Human Rights Treaties on the Domestic Level* (Kluwer Law International, 2002) 25.

60 Curious Grapevine (n 33).

resonating with a theme from literature on NGOs in international law.[61] For example, as one OHCHR staff member stated in relation to NGOs: 'The treaty bodies get both sides of the story, they [NGOs] are half of the story'. This mirrors the views of a Committee member who said: 'they're critical. At least from the perspective of the Committee in terms of their use and value to us, because without them we would only have one side of the story'. The provision of 'on the ground' or 'first-hand' information to complete the picture clearly emerged as interviewees' most valued role for NGOs.

Despite the overwhelmingly positive response to questions about the NGO role, most interviewees expressed some reservations about NGOs or about the reliability of NGO information. Scholarship on the NGO role in treaty body monitoring has not explored this reticence towards NGOs to the same degree as the positive commentary on the NGO role,[62] with the main exception of some general literature on NGO accountability.[63] In this regard, OHCHR staff and Committee members ranged from those who were sympathetic to NGOs, open to NGO reports and quite trusting of their content[64]; to those who indicated quite high levels of scepticism of NGO information and motives. However, even the latter expressed support for NGO input once it could be verified: 'Of course NGOs are important sources of information but sometimes, because they are partisans of ideas, sometimes they might be exaggerating'.[65]

The most common theme from interviews was that NGO information needed to be verified against other 'official sources' or that Committees need to be 'critical and questioning of NGO information'.[66] Two interviewees suggested that NGO information be used only in order to present that information to the State party,[67] 'not as allegations but for your response'.[68]

---

61 Laurie Wiseberg, 'Protecting Human Rights Activists and NGOs: What More Can Be Done?' (1991) 13(4) *Human Rights Quarterly* 525 ('Protecting Human Rights Activists'); Steve Charnovitz, 'Nongovernmental Organizations and International Law' (2006) 100(2) *American Journal of International Law* 348, 348.

62 See, e.g. Role of NGOs in Protection of Human Rights(n 52); Freeman (n 54).

63 Diana Hortsch, 'The Paradox of Partnership: Amnesty International, Responsible Advocacy and NGO Accountability' (2010) 42(1) *Columbian Human Rights Law Review* 119.

64 Curious Grapevine (n 33).

65 Ibid.

66 OHCHR Interviewee, interview conducted 30 April 2015, Geneva; CERD Committee Member Interviewee, interview conducted 30 April 2015; OHCHR interviewee, interview conducted 28 April 2015, Geneva.

67 CERD Committee Member Interviewee, interview conducted 30 April 2015, Geneva; OHCHR interviewee, interview conducted 28 April 2015, Geneva.

68 OHCHR interviewee, interview conducted 28 April 2015, Geneva.

In reality though, this author's observation of constructive dialogues, in Geneva and via webcasts, confirms that States are asked many questions, some of which are long statements or rhetorical questions. States do not always respond to each one, due to lack of time, lack of information to hand, or perhaps lack of willingness to respond.

At the most extreme end of the scale, some interviewees indicated that suspect NGO information is 'filtered out', that in practice, the OHCHR can exclude NGO reports to any treaty body if they are:

> unsubstantiated in any way . . . what's obviously inflammatory or politically motivated. We discount this type of information before it gets to the treaty body to prevent too much paperwork which would eat up time. If it's manifestly one-sided.[69]

Some Committee members, on the other hand, seemed unaware of the behind-the-scenes filtering by the OHCHR but applied their own filter to NGO information they did not agree with, or deemed to be lacking credibility, or coming from GONGOs. They also reported an inability to read all NGO reports; one commented: 'The problem for us, because we do have a problem, we have too much to read. At the last minute. They [NGOs] send it very late and we have more than the State party report. It's difficult for us'.[70]

A key output from the State-reporting process is the publication of concluding observations by the treaty body, which contain, *inter alia*, recommendations for States. Suggesting recommendations for concluding observations is a key opportunity for NGO influence.[71] The unique understanding and expertise of NGOs, particularly domestic NGOs, was seen as invaluable by some interviewees, particularly where they propose very specific and 'implementable' recommendations. A Government interviewee commented that NGOs often produce quality, influential reports[72]; one of them saw this as common across treaty bodies: 'That's the trend that we've seen with NGOs engaging with treaty bodies. They write really detailed shadow reports and those shadow reports are really influential on the kinds of areas that the Committees look at'.[73] Geneva-based NGO interviewees

---

69 Ibid.
70 Curious Grapevine (n 33).
71 CERD Committee Member Interviewee, interview conducted 28 April 2015, Geneva; CERD Committee Member Interviewee, interview conducted 28 April 2015, Geneva; OHCHR Interviewee interview conducted 30 April 2015, Geneva.
72 Australian Government Interviewee, interview conducted 7 January 2016, telephone interview.
73 Ibid.

identified the same trend, noting that Committee members directly use NGO information in the constructive dialogue,[74] and in the concluding observations: 'So from our perspective a key factor is the issue of credibility, so when you have an NGO that has a lot of credibility, the information will be taken as secure, and the information will be taken for granted'.[75]

There is little empirical evidence of the influence of NGOs on treaty body concluding observations, but in my previous research using an Australian case study of NGO engagement with the CERD Committee, I identified that 52 per cent of the Committee's recommendations appear to have been influenced by NGOs due to the very similar text used. More recommendations had a 'general match' with NGO reports, meaning that different language was used but the issue or the substance of the recommendation was the same, so the overall match may be as high as 81 per cent.[76] The Australian case study found that an NGO coalition report was most influential. This was a report from *domestic* NGOs, resonating with the trend both in international human rights law and in the literature, both of which have gradually moved from a focus on international NGOs to recognition of the importance of domestic NGOs, particularly in Western European and Other Group (WEOG) States. Domestic NGOs have the added advantage for the UN of acting as intermediaries so that international law can be adapted as what Merry describes as a 'localizing transnational knowledge of rights',[77] and can play a significant role in bridging the gap between international standards and local human rights issues. They also use the international system to hold their Governments to account and as such provide social accountability.[78]

Given that NGOs play a useful role, the treaty bodies and the OHCHR are likely to be reluctant to acknowledge the potential extent of NGO influence lest States protest. As one Committee member said:

> It is a delicate balancing act. There is no point in the outcome of a treaty body discussion being lauded by NGOs if it's ignored by the States

---

74 Curious Grapevine (n 33).
75 MRG international NGO Interviewee, interview conducted 29 April 2015, Geneva.
76 Fiona McGaughey, 'Advancing, Retreating or Stepping on Each Other's Toes? The Role of Non-Governmental Organisations in United Nations Human Rights Treaty Body Reporting and the Universal Periodic Review' (2018) 35 *Australian Year Book of International Law* 187, 198.
77 Sally Engle Merry, *Human Rights and Gender Violence: Translating International Law into Local Justice* (University of Chicago Press, 2006) 179.
78 Helene Grandvoinnet, Ghazia Aslam and Shomikho Raha, *Opening the Black Box: The Contextual Drivers of Social Accountability* (World Bank Group, 2015).

parties. It's essential that that balance is found and that's challenging for both NGOs and States parties.[79]

4 The role of NGOs in bringing individual complaints to treaty bodies

The treaty body individual complaint mechanisms (also called petitions or individual communications) allow individuals to bring a complaint under the human rights treaties alleging a violation of treaty rights. This is a useful tool for NGOs, particularly for strategic litigation of test cases. However, State reporting remains the most widely used mechanism and although increasing in availability, individual complaints mechanisms have not always been as widely used as we might expect.[80] They are only available as an option where the State party has accepted the authority of the treaty body to hear complaints, having ratified the relevant treaty and accepted the complaints procedure by making a declaration under the treaty or by ratifying the relevant optional protocol.[81] There are some minor procedural variations between the treaty bodies but overall the individual complaints mechanisms are very similar. At the time of writing, eight of the human rights treaty bodies (the Human Rights Committee, CERD, CAT, CEDAW, CRPD, CED, CESCR, and CRoC) may, under certain conditions, receive and consider individual complaints.[82]

Although some committees' rules of procedure provide for parties to make oral comments, individual complaints are usually considered in closed session meetings and 'on the papers' rather than relying on a trial or other face-to-face procedure. This has the benefit of being less expensive and more accessible.[83] It is possible to bring a complaint without a

---

79 CERD Committee Member Interviewee, interview conducted 27 April 2015, Geneva.

80 Phoebe Okowa, 'The International Court of Justice and the Georgia/Russia Dispute' (2011) 11(4) *Human Rights Law Review* 739.

81 *Optional Protocol to the International Covenant on Civil and Political Rights*, opened for signature 16 December 1966, 999 UNTS 171 (entered into force 23 March 1976).

82 'Human Rights Treaty Bodies – Individual Communications: Procedure for Complaints by Individuals under the Human Rights Treaties' *Office of the High Commissioner for Human Rights* (Web Page) <www.ohchr.org/EN/HRBodies/TBPetitions/Pages/IndividualCom munications.aspx#:~:text=Overview%20of%20the%20individual%20complaints%20 procedure&text=The%20basic%20concept%20of%20complaint,of%20experts%20 monitoring%20the%20treaty>.

83 Claire Callejon, Kamelia Kemileva and Felix Kirchmeier, *Treaty Bodies' Individual Communication Procedures: Providing Redress and Reparation to Victims of Human Rights Violations* (Geneva Academy of International Humanitarian Law and Human Rights, May 2019) <www.geneva-academy.ch/joomlatools-files/docman-files/UN%20Treaty%20 Bodies%20Individual%20Communications.pdf>.

lawyer although this can be challenging.[84] Callejon et al explain the procedure, including the general admissibility requirements. These are as follows: the complainant must have exhausted all domestic remedies and the *ratione personae* requirement, whereby the petitioner must show that they are directly affected by the events. This is discussed further later with regard to complaints brought by NGOs. Under the *ratione materiae* requirement, the alleged violations must fall within the scope of application of the treaty in question and under the *lis pendens* rule, the complaint must not be under examination or have been examined by another international body.[85] The *ratione temporis* requirement means that the alleged violation must have occurred after the entry into force of the complaint mechanism for the State party. Finally, some Committees have time limits, for example, communications to the Human Rights Committee may be submitted no later than five years after the exhaustion of domestic remedies or, where applicable, three years from the conclusion of another procedure of international investigation or settlement according to Rule 99(c) of its Rules of Procedure.[86]

Sękowska-Kozłowska argues that the individual communication procedure is the second most important tool available to treaty bodies (next to State reporting) but that, unlike regional mechanisms, such as the individual complaints procedure to the European Court of Human Rights, UN treaties do not specifically provide for NGO participation in individual complaint procedures.[87] Despite this, NGOs do play a role and there are opportunities for some degree of NGO participation. She identifies four different modes of NGO engagement. In the first, NGOs act as representatives of the petitioner and in the second, NGOs act as an entity submitting the communication on behalf of the victim. The third and fourth are less common – namely, NGOs acting as an entity submitting the communication on its own behalf and NGOs acting as a third party (*amicus curiae*) which is not formally provided for by the treaties.[88] The most common form of NGO engagement is the first of these – acting as a representative of the petitioner and is the only form uncontested and admitted by all the committees.[89] This is

---

84 Ibid.
85 Ibid.
86 Ibid.
87 Katarzyna Sękowska-Kozłowska, 'The Role of Non-Governmental Organisations in Individual Communication Procedures Before the UN Human Rights Treaty Bodies' in Alexander J Bělohlávek, Naděžda Rozehnalová and Filip Černý (eds), *Czech Yearbook of International Law – The Role of Governmental and Non-Governmental Organizations in the 21st Century* (Juris Publishing, 2014) 367, 369.
88 Ibid 370.
89 Ibid. Sękowska-Kozłowska notes that this role is provided for in some of the treaty bodies' rules of procedure. See, e.g. Human Rights Committee, *Rules of Procedure of the*

also supported in jurisprudence of the treaty bodies.[90] The second form of engagement is where the complaint is submitted on behalf of petitioner who is unable to submit it. These complaints are sometimes brought by family members. In this scenario, the person who has experienced the alleged human rights violation is unable to submit a complaint (e.g. due to death or disappearance) and as such is unable to give the NGO consent to act on their behalf. In this case, the NGO must justify standing to bring the complaint. The most well-known examples of this type of case are the cases of *Goecke v Austria* and *Yildirim v Austria* before the CEDAW Committee whereby in both cases the petitioner had been killed by their partner and the case was brought by an NGO on behalf of their children, alleging that the State Party failed to provide appropriate protection to victims of domestic violence.[91]

Taking into account the need to have exhausted domestic remedies, the individual complaints procedures do not constitute a rapid remedy for those who have had their rights violated but, as mentioned earlier, can be useful for strategic litigation in areas of systematic rights violation.[92] A key challenge can be the non-binding nature of the Committees' Final Views (decisions) and in some cases, States' failure to implement the Committees' decisions and to give remedy. For example, NGO Remedy Australia reports that of the 40 complaints against Australia to UN treaty bodies, only five (12.5 per cent) have been fully remedied in accordance with the Committee's Final Views.[93]

Human Rights Committee, UN Doc CCPR/C/3/Rev.11 (9 January 2019); Committee on the Elimination of Discrimination against Women, *Rules of Procedure of the Committee on the Elimination of Discrimination against Women*, UN Doc CEDAW/C/ROP (26 January 2001).

90 Sękowska-Kozłowska (n 92) 370–1. Sękowska-Kozłowska refers to, for example: views of the Human Rights Committee ('HRC') in HRC, *Llantoy Huaman v Peru: Communication No. 1153/2003*, 85th sess, UN Doc CCPR/C/85/D/1153/2003 (24 October 2005); Committee on the Elimination of All Forms of Racial Discrimination, *Adan v Denmark: Communication No. 43/2008*, 77th sess, UN Doc CERD/C/77/D/43/2008 (13 August 2010); views of CAT in Committee Against Torture, *Ristic v Yugoslavia: Communication No. 113/1998*, 22nd sess, UN Doc CAT/C/26/D/113/1998 (11 May 2011); views of CEDAW in Committee on the Elimination of Discrimination Against Women, *AS v Hungary: Communication No. 4/2004*, 36th sess, UN Doc CEDAW/C/36/D/4/2004 (14 August 2006).

91 Committee on the Elimination of Discrimination Against Women, *Goecke v Austria, Communication No. 5/2005*, 39th sess, UN Doc CEDAW/C/39/D/5/2005 (6 August 2007); Committee on the Elimination of Discrimination Against Women, *Yildirim v Austria, Communication No. 6/2005*, 39th sess, UN Doc CEDAW/C/39/D/6/2005 (6 August 2007).

92 The case of *Toonen v Australia* being a good example of this: Human Rights Committee, *Toonen v Australia: Communication No. 488/1992*, 50th sess, UN Doc CCPR/C/50/D/488/1992 (31 March 1994).

93 Remedy Australia, *Follow-Up Report on Violations by Australia of ICCPR in Individual Communications (1994–2017)* (October 2017) <https://remedy.org.au/reports/2017_RemedyAustralia_Follow-Up_Report_on_individual_communications.pdf>.

Nonetheless, for many people, having their case heard by a UN body, even if not ultimately remedied, can be a powerful experience. Ball's research on individual complaints to UN treaty bodies found that whether treaty bodies' views are implemented or not, they bear witness to violations and offer validation, dignity, self-respect, and moral support to petitioners.[94]

Finally, there are additional complaints mechanisms available to NGOs through the Human Rights Council, discussed in the following chapter.

5 Conclusion

NGOs fought for inclusion in the drafting of the UN Charter, resulting in Article 71 of the Charter which provides for consultation with NGOs. They went on to contribute to the drafting of the UDHR and to human rights treaties, and later to informing the interpretation of treaties through their contribution to treaty body general comments and general recommendations. Their contemporary role extends well beyond the drafting of treaties. As discussed here, NGOs play an essential governance role in holding governments to account on their human rights treaty obligations. They do so in two main ways. The first is by providing information and suggesting recommendations to UN treaty bodies. The information supplements reports provided by governments so that the Committee of independent experts can better assess the actual state of human rights on the ground. The second is by bringing individual complaints to treaty bodies, most commonly as representatives of the petitioner or as an entity submitting the communication on behalf of the victim. UN staff and treaty body members strongly value the NGO role, seeing it as ranging from 'important' to 'absolutely crucial'. This resonates with Wiseberg's assertion that the UN human rights machinery 'would grind to a halt were it not fed by the fact-finding of human rights NGOs'.[95]

94 Olivia Ball, *All the Way to the UN: Is Petitioning a UN Human-rights Treaty Body Worthwhile?* (PhD Thesis, Monash University, 2014).
95 Protecting Human Rights Activists (n 61) 525.

5 NGOs and the Human Rights Council

1 Introduction

Chapter 4 outlined the significant role played by NGOs in the UN treaty bodies; this chapter examines the NGO role in the Human Rights Council (HRC). The HRC is the primary human rights body at the UN but treaty bodies have responsibility for the monitoring of implementation of the treaties. The HRC and treaty bodies should be viewed by NGOs as complementary. The HRC was established by resolution 60/251 in 2006 to replace the UN Commission on Human Rights.[1] The Commission was accused of political bias in the selection of states for scrutiny and a lack of credibility and professionalism.[2] In resolution 60/251 establishing the HRC, the General Assembly acknowledged the important role played by NGOs and other civil society actors in the promotion and protection of human rights. NGOs can observe sessions of the HRC and have some opportunities for participation. It is increasingly possible for those wishing to stay abreast of the work of the HRC to follow online, including through the website and webcasts.[3]

This chapter discusses the various ways in which NGOs can substantively engage with the HRC, beginning with an overview of the NGO role in the HRC, then their role in the key monitoring mechanism of the HRC – the Universal Periodic Review. This is followed by a discussion of the NGO role in the work of the Special Procedures mandate holders; in HRC

---

1 *Human Rights Council,* GA Res 60/251, UN GAOR, 60th sess, 72nd plen mtg, Agenda Items 46 and 120, UN Doc A/RES/60/251 (3 April 2006).

2 UN Secretary General, *In Larger Freedom: Development, Security, and Respect for Human Rights,* 59th sess, Agenda Items 45 and 55, UN Doc A/59/2005 (26 May 2005) para 4 ('*In Larger Freedom*').

3 *United Nations Human Rights Council* (website) <www.ohchr.org/EN/HRBodies/HRC/Pages/Home.aspx>.

complaints mechanisms; in the HRC Advisory Committee; and finally, the NGO opportunities in other HRC working groups and fora.

2 NGO participation in the Human Rights Council

The HRC is generally perceived to be open and accessible to NGOs. ECOSOC accreditation is required for NGO observers to HRC sessions and by registering in advance, those with ECOSOC status may make oral interventions in HRC general debates and interactive dialogues, although not during the Universal Periodic Review, as discussed in the next section. Landolt and Woo's empirical analysis comparing NGO statements to the Commission with statements to the HRC indicates that NGO participation is increasing in the HRC, compared with the Commission and that this is particularly the case among domestic, regional, and Southern NGOs.[4]

Depending on their ECOSOC accreditation status, NGOs can engage with the HRC by attending sessions, submitting written statements, making oral statements, holding side events, and even participating in informal negotiations on Council resolutions. The International Service for Human Rights (ISHR) notes that NGOs successfully influenced the HRC members to conduct an inquiry into alleged war crimes and crimes against humanity in Sri Lanka.[5] NGOs also pushed for a commission of inquiry into the Democratic People's Republic of Korea, enabling 'victims' to give the HRC a first-hand account of the atrocities, ultimately, leading to a referral of the human rights situation to the UN Security Council.[6]

3 The Universal Periodic Review (UPR) and NGOs[7]

Up until 2008, the key State-reporting mechanisms were those of UN human rights treaty bodies, as described in the previous chapter. Since 2008, these existing mechanisms have been supplemented by the 'cornerstone of the

---

4 Laura K Landolt and Byungwon Woo, 'NGOs Invite Attention: From the United Nations Commission on Human Rights to the Human Rights Council' (2017) 16(4) *Journal of Human Rights* 407.

5 Tess McEvoy and Juli King, 'Submission to report of High Commissioner on Civil society space in multilateral institutions: Existing Interaction, Challenges, Good Practice & Recommendations' (International Service for Human Rights, October 2017) 6.

6 Ibid.

7 Some of this section has been adapted from: Fiona McGaughey, 'The Role and Influence of Non-Governmental Organisations in the Universal Periodic Review – International Context and Australian Case Study' (2017) 17(3) *Human Rights Law Review* 421.

Human Rights Council's institution building package',[8] the Universal Periodic Review ('UPR'). Whereas the nine core UN human rights treaties cover thematic areas, such as civil and political rights, torture, or children's rights and are entered into by States voluntarily, the UPR applies to *all* 193 UN member States and covers *all* aspects of a State's human rights obligations. While the functions of UN treaty bodies and Special Procedures mandates are performed by independent experts, the UPR is a peer-review mechanism – States hold each other to account on their human rights records. The review is based on three reports: a report from the State-under-Review, a compilation of UN information, and a *stakeholder summary report*. The stakeholder summary report is where submissions by NGOs are reflected. These written submissions and the lobbying of States prior to the review are the key ways in which NGOs can engage with the UPR.

As discussed in the previous chapter, it has been claimed that NGOs play an essential role in treaty body State reporting, but the same claims of importance of the NGO role in the UPR have not yet been made, or at least not to the same extent. Initially when modalities were still being refined, there was something of a 'honeymoon period', where States and other key actors showed initial enthusiasm about the HRC and its UPR. This included optimism that the UPR would offer unique opportunities for NGOs to bring human rights issues of concern to the attention of the international community and to engage in associated advocacy at a national level. For example, Schokman and Lynch stated:

> The UPR has attracted a great deal of attention since it commenced in 2008. From an NGO perspective, this excitement flows from the new and high profile opportunities for NGOs to advocate for the improved protection and promotion of human rights on the ground.[9]

Yet, as well as being an opportunity, in some ways the NGO role in the UPR is quite limited. As a State-led peer-review mechanism, rather than a review by independent experts, certain States can be resistant to NGOs

---

8 Human Rights Council, *Institution-Building of the United Nations Human Rights Council*, 5th sess, 9th mtg, UN Doc A/HRC/RES/5/1 (18 June 2007) ('*Institution-Building of HRC*').

9 Ben Schokman and Phil Lynch, 'Effective NGO Engagement with the Universal Periodic Review' in Hilary Charlesworth and Emma Larking (eds), *Human Rights and the Universal Periodic Review: Rituals and Ritualism* (Cambridge University Press, 2015) 126, 126. See also Lawrence C Moss, 'Opportunities for Nongovernmental Organization Advocacy in the Universal Periodic Review Process at the UN Human Rights Council' (2010) 2(1) *Journal of Human Rights Practice* 122.

and their criticism.[10] It is not surprising that in the UN State-centric system there are limitations to what NGOs can do as they are 'a continual source of controversy and irritation' for Governments.[11] Yet, civil society engagement is essential for the mechanism. In Charlesworth and Larking's seminal work on the UPR, *Human Rights and the Universal Periodic Review: Rituals and Ritualism*,[12] they note that 'The ability of the UPR to transcend ritualism and to function as an empowering regulatory mechanism depends heavily on effective NGO and civil society engagement in the process'.[13]

When the modalities of the UPR were being developed, the African Group argued that NGOs should have no role at all in the HRC, including the UPR.[14] Jordaan notes that, although not all of the recommendations made by the African Group in this regard were taken on board, the resultant UPR mechanism put States in a very dominant position.[15] Perhaps because of the quite limited NGO role, many NGOs have been able to participate relatively unfettered in the UPR. However, other NGOs have been prevented from attending the HRC, or managed to participate but suffered intimidation and reprisals as a result.[16]

It is clear that the HRC is a political body and that NGOs, Governments, and other stakeholders engaging with the UPR require more than a simply legal approach. Compared with the treaty bodies for example, the UPR process requires NGOs not only to engage with the legal human rights provisions but also to use politics, diplomacy, and/or international relations to lobby for change. As Schokman and Lynch state: 'The inherently political nature of the UPR continues to provide the biggest opportunity for achieving significant human rights change on the ground, but also remains the biggest challenge for NGOs'.[17]

---

10 Rachel Brett, 'The Role of NGOs: An Overview' in Gudmundur Alfredsson et al (eds), *International Human Rights Monitoring Mechanisms Essays in Honour of Jakob Th. Möller* (Martinus Nijhoff, 2nd rev ed, 2009) 673.

11 Ibid 674.

12 Hilary Charlesworth and Emma Larking (eds), *Human Rights and the Universal Periodic Review: Rituals and Ritualism* (Cambridge University Press, 2015).

13 Hilary Charlesworth and Emma Larking, 'Introduction: The Regulatory Power of the Universal Periodic Review' in Charlesworth and Larking(eds) (n 12) 1, 16.

14 Eduard Jordaan, 'South Africa and the United Nations Human Rights Council' (2014) 36(1) *Human Rights Quarterly* 90, 120.

15 Ibid 121.

16 See, e.g. reports of reprisals in UN Secretary General, *Cooperation with the United Nations, its Representatives and Mechanisms in the Field of Human Rights*, 30th sess, Agenda Items 2 and 5, UN Doc A/HRC/30/29 (17 August 2015).

17 Schokman and Lynch (n 9).

NGO participation in the UPR is provided for in HRC Resolution 5/1 which established the UPR.[18] It is no coincidence that NGOs were also more active in drafting this resolution than they had been, for example, in discussions on the review of the former Sub-Commission or the '1503' complaints procedure under the Commission.[19]

3.1 NGO reporting in the UPR

NGO reports balance the information provided by States by raising human rights issues that may have been avoided – or misrepresented – in State reports, or by expanding on issues acknowledged in State reports. However, unlike UN treaty body reviews, in the UPR NGOs do not always have the benefit of having seen the Government report and responding to it.[20] NGO reports must be submitted in advance of the Government report, at least five months before the relevant session of the UPR Working Group.[21] Individual NGO submissions to the UPR should not exceed 2,815 words and submissions from coalitions should not exceed 5,630 words.[22] This is clearly an extremely tight word limit to cover all human rights issues within each State. The OHCHR guidelines state that 'Joint submissions by a large number of stakeholders are encouraged',[23] and Schokman and Lynch concluded from their experience that a coordinated and strategic NGO coalition is key to effective engagement with the UPR.[24] In my previous research, interview data and case studies also testify to the effectiveness of coordinated and strategic NGO coalitions.

18 *Institution-Building of HRC*, UN Doc A/HRC/RES/5/1(n 8) para 3(m).
19 Gareth Sweeney and Yuri Saito, 'An NGO Assessment of the New Mechanisms of the UN Human Rights Council' (2009) 9(2) *Human Rights Law Review*203.
20 Whether NGOs see the State report in advance, and whether they see a draft or final version, depends on the State under Review. States are encouraged to consult with civil society in drafting their report. See the guidelines adopted at the 6th HRC session in September 2007: Human Rights Council, *Follow-up to Human Rights Council Resolution 5/1*, 6th sess, 20th mtg, UN Doc A/HRC/DEC/6/102 (27 September 2007). They were modified for the second and subsequent UPR cycles by Human Rights Council, *Follow-Up to the Human Rights Council Resolution 16/21 with Regard to the Universal Periodic Review*, UN GAOR, 17th sess, 35th mtg, Agenda Item 1, UN Doc A/HRC/DEC/17/119 (19 July 2011).
21 Office of the High Commissioner for Human Rights, *Universal Periodic Review: Information and Guidelines for Relevant Stakeholders' Written Submissions* (17 March 2015), para 27 <www.ohchr.org/Documents/HRBodies/UPR/TechnicalGuideEN.pdf> ('*UPR Information and Guidelines for Written Submissions*').
22 Ibid.
23 Ibid para 23.
24 Schokman and Lynch(n 9) 133.

Submissions received by NGOs and National Human Rights Institutions ('NHRIs') are then summarised by the UPR Secretariat into a ten-page stakeholder summary report. This forms one of the three official UN reports on which the UPR is based and as such it is important for NGOs that their content is reflected in this report. The OHCHR technical guidelines for stakeholder submissions encourage submissions which, *inter alia*, contain credible and reliable information, highlight main issues of concern, and identify possible recommendations.[25]

However, Billaud's ethnographic study of the UPR exposed that there are other criteria for submissions, not made public, and that these are constantly negotiated and re-interpreted by those drafting the stakeholder summary reports.[26] For example, priority may be given to NGOs with ECOSOC accreditation, even though this is not required to submit a report, and NGO contributions may be excluded if they are not of a particular standard or are not written in an official UN language,[27] effectively limiting NGO input and likely disproportionately those from the Global South. The covert rules and politicised nature of the UPR also mean that reports by GONGOs, or Government-friendly organisations, could be included in the stakeholder summary report.[28] The lack of transparency described by Billaud is concerning. Given the criticisms of the HRC's predecessor, the UN Human Rights Commission, including political bias in the selection of States for scrutiny and lack of credibility and professionalism,[29] transparent guidelines and working methods in the UPR are important for the legitimacy of the HRC.

3.2 NGO consultation and lobbying in the UPR

NGOs do not have a formal opportunity to brief recommending States as part of the UPR – they can merely make a two-minute statement before the adoption of the final report of the Working Group.[30] Instead, NGOs carry out informal lobbying outside of the HRC meetings. Given the peer-review

---

25 *UPR Information and Guidelines for Written Submissions* (n 21) 3.
26 Julie Billaud, 'Keepers of the Truth: Producing 'Transparent' Documents for the Universal Periodic Review' in Charlesworth and Larking (eds) (n 12) 63, 70.
27 Ibid.
28 Ibid 68.
29 *In Larger Freedom*, UN Doc A/59/2005(n 2).
30 Office of the High Commissioner for Human Rights, *A Practical Guide for Civil Society: How to Follow Up on United Nations Human Rights Recommendations*, 4, <www.ohchr. org/Documents/AboutUs/CivilSociety/HowtoFollowUNHRRecommendations.pdf> (*'Practical Guide for Civil Society'*).

and more politicised nature of the UPR compared with other UN human rights bodies, NGOs' ability to lobby States – rather than influence independent experts at the UN – is an important skill and one that many NGOs have had to develop.[31]

There are consultation and lobbying opportunities at both a national and international level. These opportunities are seen as alternatives to addressing the HRC's UPR working group. Along with word limits, some interviewees in my research identified this as a key restriction of the UPR. States are encouraged to engage civil society in consultations in the drafting of the national report.[32] NGOs can also use recommendations from the UPR in their national advocacy work and can play a role in monitoring progress on the State's implementation of the recommendations.[33]

International lobbying takes place in three main ways – NGOs can engage with embassies in their own country, they can lobby missions in Geneva, and they can attend UPR-Info's pre-sessions. However, face-to-face lobbying may change dramatically in light of COVID-19. Pre-sessions bring together embassy staff from the Permanent Missions in Geneva, NGOs, and NHRIs to discuss the human rights situation of the States under review, one month prior to their review. These sessions present a unique lobbying opportunity for NGOs.[34] Some civil society actors use the UPR-Info database of recommendations to develop a targeted approach,[35] identifying which States are interested in particular human rights issues based on their previous recommendations. They can also identify and seek to influence those States which have made recommendations which the State under review did not accept, or did not implement. This type of comprehensive database is quite unique in UN human rights bodies and is advantageous to many actors.

In the first empirical study on the UPR in 2010, Moss identified that the UPR presented opportunities for NGOs, not only by engaging in Geneva but also by using the UPR as a lobbying tool domestically.[36] He analysed the reviews of 16 States in the UPR's second cycle and concluded that NGOs had had considerable success in influencing the recommendations made in the UPR, but that States were more resistant to accepting these recommendations.[37] The second analysis of NGO influence was the more comprehensive study in 2013 by McMahon et al examining UPR sessions 3–13 from

31   Schokman and Lynch(n 9).
32   *Institution-Building of HRC*, UN Doc A/HRC/RES/5/1(n 8).
33   *Practical Guide for Civil Society*(n 30) 48–9.
34   UPR-Info, *Pre-sessions*, <www.upr-info.org/en/upr-process/pre-sessions>.
35   UPR-Info, *Database of Recommendations*, <www.upr-info.org/database/>.
36   Moss (n 9).
37   Ibid 123.

December 2008 to May 2012.[38] They also found that civil society organisation recommendations were reflected in State recommendations (at a rate of 67 per cent). Contrary to Moss' findings, McMahon's study concluded that civil society organisation-suggested recommendations were slightly *more* likely to be accepted by the State. It is possible that one reason for the difference is that McMahon's study included both NGO and NHRI recommendations but it is unclear whether Moss' did as he refers only to NGOs.

My case study of Australia's UPR in 2015 found that although NGOs did influence recommendations made by States, the most influential source of recommendations was the compilation of UN information report.[39] A total of 197 of the 290 recommendations made to Australia by other States (68 per cent) had either a general or specific match to the recommendations contained in this report. Of these 197 recommendations, 58 of them were the *unique* source for the recommendation made by the State in the UPR – meaning the recommendation had not also been made by the NHRI or NGOs. The second most influential source was NGO submissions from the stakeholder summary report with 177 of the 290 recommendations made by States (61 per cent) having either a general or specific match to the recommendations contained in this report. Thirty-three of these 177 recommendations were the unique source for the recommendations made by States.

Although it then seems that the compilation of UN information report is more influential than the NGO information in the stakeholder summary report, it is not quite that straightforward. This report provides recommendations from treaty bodies, Special Rapporteurs, and others but NGOs can also influence the recommendations made by those UN human rights bodies. Where these recommendations were relied upon in the UPR, some were originally informed by NGOs.[40]

The question of what *types* of NGO are most influential in the UPR has also been considered. Moss analysed which NGOs were more likely to have their content reflected in the stakeholder summary report and found that it was INGOs with ECOSOC accreditation[41] (supporting Billaud's claim that

---

38 McMahon et al, *The Universal Periodic Review, Do Civil Society Organization-Suggested Recommendations Matter?* (Dialogue on Globalization, Friedrich-Ebert-Stiftung, November 2013). 'Civil society organisations' is a broader term than NGOs and includes, *inter alia*, NGOs, human rights defenders, victim groups, faith-based groups, unions, and research institutes such as universities: Office of the High Commissioner for Human Rights, *Working with the United Nations Human Rights Programme: A Handbook for Civil Society*, UN Doc HR/PUB/06/10/Rev.1 (2008) vii ('*Civil Society Handbook*').

39 McGaughey (n 7).

40 Ibid 444.

41 Moss (n 9).

preference was given to content from NGOs with ECOSOC accreditation in the stakeholder summary). This was followed by national NGOs without ECOSOC accreditation. In the Australian case study, one NGO coalition clearly emerged as the most influential – a domestic coalition whose report was endorsed by over 190 NGOs and civil society organisations. One possible reason for the difference in Moss' finding that international NGOs were more influential and the contrary finding in the Australian case study is that international NGOs may be more important in reviews of less democratic States with a restricted civil society. In a WEOG (Western European and Others Group) State, such as Australia, domestic NGOs may be more significant.[42] Given the opportunities for NGOs to engage with follow-up on the implementation of recommendations, the prevalence of a strong domestic NGO coalition is useful. Merry argues that domestic NGOs have the added advantage for the UN of acting as intermediaries so that international law can be adapted as a 'localizing transnational knowledge of rights'.[43]

A unique feature of the UPR is that in the weeks following the review, the State can choose whether they accept the recommendations. It could be argued that this weakens the effectiveness of the review. However, internationally, 74 per cent of all recommendations made in the UPR were found to be accepted by States.[44] Research has found that Governments may be more likely to accept NGO-influenced recommendations.[45] There are a number of possible reasons for this finding, including the potential for domestic NGOs to effectively act in their intermediary role by suggesting recommendations that are both compliant with international law and suited to the local context.[46] NGOs have considerable skills and knowledge which they bring to bear in influencing UN human rights bodies,[47] therefore, NGOs, rather than UN bodies, may develop the most appropriate recommendations, more likely to be accepted by the State under review.

A recurrent theme in the interviews I carried out was the opportunity that the UPR had created to develop closer working relationships between key

42 See, e.g. Sally Engle Merry, *Human Rights and Gender Violence: Translating International Law into Local Justice* (University of Chicago Press, 2006); Beth A Simmons, *Mobilizing for Human Rights: International Law in Domestic Politics* (Cambridge University Press, 2009).

43 Merry (n 42) 179.

44 UPR-Info, *Beyond Promises: The Impact of the UPR on the Ground* (2014) <www.upr-info.org/sites/default/files/general-document/pdf/2014_beyond_promises.pdf>.

45 McGaughey (n 7) 447–9; McMahon et al (n 38).

46 Merry (n 42) 179.

47 See, e.g. Kerstin Martens, 'Professionalised Representation of Human Rights NGOs to the United Nations' (2006) 10(1) *The International Journal of Human Rights* 19.

actors. The growth in NGOs and international NGOs engaging with each other to advance the human rights agenda has been well documented.[48] This is also the case in the UPR, but the UPR is creating or bolstering three other types of relationship; firstly, the relationship between NGOs and the State, secondly the relationship between civil society and international diplomats, and finally the relationship between NGOs themselves.

The former Executive Director of UPR-Info reflected that the UPR had 'pushed NGOs and governments to sit down together to discuss human rights' and that most states hold national consultations (80 per cent in the second cycle).[49] He also noted that the UPR had 'pushed NGOs to form coalitions and start working for the first time together, while they did not have that opportunity in the past because they were working on different issues'.

Some interviewees noted that it was mutually agreeable for international NGOs to submit their own reports rather than join the coalition, for example, because it was their policy internationally. There were also reports of international NGOs acting as the spokesperson on behalf of domestic NGOs. In this case, coalitions of domestic NGOs and international NGOs emerged as particularly important where there is a repressive regime. Where domestic NGOs cannot openly criticise their Government, international NGOs are an important conduit for their information. As the Executive Director of Geneva-based ISHR explained: 'in those cases we will put in the submission in our own name with no reference to the national level partner or "informant" because to name them would be to put them at risk of reprisal.'[50]

NGO coalitions are actively encouraged by the UPR Working Group, but of course forming a cohesive, coordinated NGO coalition, where diverse interests and issues are accommodated, can be challenging. This is even more pronounced in the UPR than in other mechanisms given the breadth of topics for consideration and the very tight word limit for reports. The relationship between domestic and international NGOs can also be challenging.

Some international NGOs have been criticised for submitting their own report without any knowledge of issues on the ground, or engagement with domestic NGOs.[51] Furthermore, at the one formal opportunity to brief the

---

48 Margaret E Keck and Kathryn Sikkink, *Activists Beyond Borders: Advocacy Networks in International Politics* (Cornell University Press, 1st ed, 1998); Thomas Risse, Stephen C Ropp and Kathryn Sikkink (eds), *The Power of Human Rights, International Norms and Domestic Change* (Cambridge University Press, 1999).

49 McGaughey (n 7) 434.

50 Ibid 436.

51 See, e.g. Natalie Baird, 'The Role of International Non-Governmental Organisations in the Universal Periodic Review of Pacific Island States: Can "Doing Good" Be Done Better?' (2015) 16(2) *Melbourne Journal of International Law* 550.

HRC at the adoption of the working group's report, it has been noted that this opportunity can be dominated by international NGOs and that Geneva-based NGOs with the institutional knowledge and benefits of being in the same time zone were first to be allocated speaking slots. For example, in my Australian case study, an Indigenous representative body did not get a speaking slot. These tensions resonate with Baird's findings that international NGOs in Pacific Island States' UPRs may have had a distorting effect on the interactive dialogue and may have diluted the voice of domestic civil society actors.[52]

UPR-Info is an interesting development in the NGO domain. Unlike some of the international NGOs which were perceived to encroach on the space of domestic NGOs, they are quite clear that they do not engage in advocacy:

> Our primary role is to provide information, not just to NGOs but to all actors in the UPR, and to monitor the UPR process . . . we also play a role as facilitator between NGOs and governments. We do not advocate for certain issues and we aim to work on every country and in that sense the countries see us as a neutral actor. And so do NGOs so we can then build trust between the stakeholders.[53]

This type of international facilitative NGO does exist in other UN human rights mechanisms, such as some of the NGOs working closely with treaty bodies and coordinating NGO engagement with them as discussed briefly in the previous chapter. However, by carefully maintaining State engagement, refraining from advocacy and managing NGO engagement and input at pre-sessions, the unique gatekeeper role played by UPR-Info in the pre-sessions is partly a result of the peer-review nature of the UPR. Although the concept of a 'gatekeeper' NGO could have some negative connotations, with 193 UN member States participating in the UPR, each with multiple stakeholder groups, a gatekeeper may be essential to the effective functioning of the UPR.[54]

4 Special procedures

Another significant mechanism of the HRC is the Special Procedures function. Special Procedures were established by the former Commission and

---

52   Ibid.
53   McGaughey (n 7) 437.
54   The Secretariat also plays a gatekeeper role in producing the stakeholder summary report and in allocating speaking time for NGOs at the adoption of the reports.

retained by the HRC. The mandate holders are independent experts known as 'Special Rapporteurs' and have either a country mandate, for example, the Special Rapporteur on the situation of human rights in Cambodia and the Special Rapporteur on the situation of human rights in Eritrea, or a thematic mandate, for example, the Special Rapporteur on the right to development and the Special Rapporteur on trafficking in persons, especially women and children. There are also working groups, such as Working Group of Experts on People of African Descent. There are 44 thematic and 12 country mandates.[55] The HRC's Institution-building package expressly provides that NGOs, as well as Governments and others, can nominate candidates as Special Procedures mandate-holders.[56]

Like most other UN bodies, the Special Rapporteurs can benefit from the critical, 'on the ground' information provided by NGOs – however, this remains somewhat under-explored in academic scholarship. The Special Rapporteurs themselves have illustrated the importance of NGOs to their work by taking their information on board for further scrutiny and using it in reports. Further, several have commented about the relevance of NGOs for their work and the importance of engagement with them. For example, in 2015, then Special Rapporteur on Violence Against Women, Professor Rashida Manjoo, made the following observation in regard to a question about the highlights of her mandate:

> The other very positive aspect has been civil society engagement. That has formed a huge part of my mandate, not only during country missions but also, more broadly, through receiving complaints,[57] holding consultations and attending conferences. The constant interaction with individuals, academic institutions and NGOs has been a source of amazing interactions, contributing to my understanding and knowledge development. I really appreciated the civil society responsiveness to me personally and to the work of my mandate in particular.[58]

In a similar vein, analysis of the work of Special Rapporteurs on Torture over a 25-year period found that the Special Rapporteurs had communicated

---

55 Office of the High Commissioner for Human Rights, *Special Procedures of the Human Rights Council: Introduction* <www.ohchr.org/EN/HRBodies/SP/Pages/Introduction. aspx>.

56 *Institution-Building of HRC*, UN Doc A/HRC/RES/5/1(n 8) para 42.

57 See ibid Part IV.

58 Rashida Manjoo and Daniela Nadj, ' "Bridging the Divide": An Interview with Professor Rashida Manjoo, UN Special Rapporteur on Violence Against Women' (2015) 23(3) *Feminist Legal Studies* 329, 341.

with many groups before, during and after a fact finding mission.[59] These groups included professional bodies, NGOs, 'victims' and their families, prison inmates, and other detainees. Engagement with them offered more direct knowledge of cases and situations falling within the mandate and the ability to identify the measures to prevent the recurrence of such cases. The Special Rapporteurs sustained working relationship with these groups, making it easier to continue to monitor situations for follow-up reporting purposes.[60]

The primary activities of Special Procedures where NGOs can have influence are: during country visits, in individual cases of alleged violations or broader structural issues, in thematic studies, as delegates in expert consultations, and by informing annual reports.[61] Paulo Sergio Pinheiro, who has held a number of Special Rapporteur positions, noted that the presentation of the reports of the Special Procedures at the UN used to be a hollow ritual, without debate, but this changed when presentation of reports became an 'interactive dialogue'.[62] He explains that initially, only member states participated but 'happily this interaction was opened to the participation of NGOs'.[63]

NGOs are referenced in the *Code of Conduct for Special Procedures Mandate-holders of the Human Rights Council*.[64] Firstly, the preamble states: 'Considering that it is necessary to assist all stakeholders, including States, national human rights institutions, non-governmental organizations and individuals, to better understand and support the activities of mandate-holders', thus identifying that NGOs are important 'supporters' of the mandates. Nonetheless, the State-centrism referred to above with regard to the UPR is strong here too, as the preamble also states:

> Considering also that such a code of conduct will strengthen the capacity of mandate-holders to exercise their functions whilst enhancing their moral authority and credibility and will require supportive action by other stakeholders, *and in particular by States*.

> (emphasis added)

59 Amrita Mukherjee, 'The Fact-Finding Missions of the Special Rapporteur on Torture' (2011) 15(2) *The International Journal of Human Rights* 265, 267.

60 Ibid.

61 All mandate holders report annually to the HRC, most also report annually to the General Assembly.

62 Paulo Sergio Pinheiro, 'Being a Special Rapporteur: A Delicate Balancing Act' (2011) 15(2) *The International Journal of Human Rights* 162, 169.

63 Ibid.

64 Human Rights Council, *Code of Conduct for Special Procedures Mandate-Holders of the Human Rights Council*, 5th sess, 9th mtg, UN Doc A/HRC/RES/5/2 (18 June 2007).

With regard to field visits, Article 11 (e) explicitly acknowledges that the Special Rapporteur should 'Seek to establish a dialogue with the relevant government authorities and with all other stakeholders'. As noted with regard to the UPR, NGOs are commonly accepted to be 'stakeholders'. The code of conduct prohibits undue pressure, gifts, or favours from governments, NGOs, or others.[65] The NGO role in submitting communications to the Special Rapporteurs is also provided for (discussed in Section 5). Special Rapporteurs will often post a 'call for inputs' on their website when they are preparing for a country visit or a thematic or annual report, representing a useful opportunity for NGOs to provide input.

In addition to this Code of Conduct, HRC resolutions relating to Special Procedures may cite engagement with civil society or NGOs. For example, the Special Rapporteur on Contemporary Forms of Slavery is required by Resolution 6/14 to:

> Request, receive and exchange information on contemporary forms of slavery from Governments, treaty bodies, special procedures, specialized agencies, intergovernmental organizations, and non-governmental organizations and other sources.[66]

A significant Special Procedure for NGOs in particular is the 'Special Rapporteur on the situation of human rights defenders'. This mandate was established by the Commission in 2000 to promote the effective implementation of the UN Declaration on Human Rights Defenders. The mandate is also responsible for studying developments and challenges on the right to promote and protect human rights; seeking and responding to information on the situation of human rights defenders; recommending effective strategies to better protect human rights defenders; and integrating a gender perspective.[67] The Special Rapporteur's annual report published in 2018 noted that the mandate holder had:

> prioritised meeting with human rights defenders around the world, formally, as part of structured consultations on his reports and activities, and informally. These encounters and commitment to listening to their voice and plights both ensure the accuracy and currency of

---

65 Ibid art 3(f), art 3(j).

66 Human Rights Council, *Special Rapporteur on Contemporary Forms of Slavery*, 6th sess, 21st mtg, UN Doc A/HRC/RES/6/14 (28 September 2007) art 2(c).

67 Commission on Human Rights, *Human Right Defenders*, 56th sess, 65th mtg, UN Doc E/CN.4/RES/2000/61 (27 April 2000).

his interventions and express his support for and solidarity with their struggles.[68]

The mandate was renewed by the HRC in 2020 and represents an important opportunity for NGO engagement.[69] Geneva-based NGO 'International Service for Human Rights' (ISHR) is active in empowering, supporting, and protecting human rights defenders.[70] Of course, the importance of protecting and promoting unfettered civil society actors is within the remit of all Special Rapporteurs given the important role NGOs and other actors play. For example, the UN Special Rapporteur on Cambodia was credited with dissuading the government of Cambodia from enacting a restrictive law on NGOs.[71]

5 Complaint procedures

Chapter 4 discussed NGO engagement with the individual complaint procedure of the treaty bodies. There are two additional complaint procedures available through the HRC – individual communications under the Special Procedures, and the HRC complaint procedure. Complaints to the Special Procedures relate to their specific thematic or geographic mandates and are submitted by or on behalf of individuals. The HRC's complaint procedure on the other hand is not for individuals but rather addresses consistent patterns of gross and reliably attested violations of all human rights and all fundamental freedoms occurring in any part of the world and under any circumstances.[72] Let's discuss the Special Procedures' complaint mechanism first.

It is quite common for NGOs, lawyers, or other civil society actors to submit complaints on behalf of individuals and sometimes these actors do so for strategic litigation purposes. Given that both the treaty bodies and the HRC's Special Procedures have individual complaint mechanisms, NGOs should consider the differences between the two mechanisms in deciding

---

68 Special Rapporteur on the Situation of Human Rights Defenders, *Report of the Special Rapporteur on the Situation of Human Rights Defenders*, 73rd sess, Agenda Item 74(b), UN Doc A/73/215 (23 July 2018) ('*Situation of Human Rights Defenders*').

69 Human Rights Council, *Decision adopted by the Human Rights Council on 13 March 2020*, 43rd sess, 34th mtg, UN Doc A/HRC/DEC/43/115 (16 March 2020).

70 See *International Service for Human Rights* <www.ishr.ch/>.

71 Surya P Subedi, 'The UN Human Rights Special Rapporteurs and the Impact of their Work: Some Reflections of the UN Special Rapporteur for Cambodia' (2016) 6(1) *Asian Journal of International Law* 1, 10.

72 *Institution-Building of HRC*, UN Doc A/HRC/RES/5/1(n 8) Part IV.

where a complaint should be lodged. The following paragraph summarises aspects of the special procedures complaints procedure, with a particular focus on aspects that differ from that of treaty bodies.

A number of the Special Procedures allow for individual complaints or a more general pattern of human rights abuse. Special Procedure complaints can be useful for critical cases as they allow for urgent or preventive action ('urgent appeals').

> Mandate-holders may resort to urgent appeals in cases where the alleged violations are time-sensitive in terms of involving loss of life, life-threatening situations, or either imminent or ongoing damage of a very grave nature to victims that cannot be addressed in a timely manner by the procedure under article 9 of the present Code.[73]

Individual complaints to Special Procedures are confidential. Also, a complaint can be made irrespective of the State in which the violation occurred – even if the State has not ratified human rights treaties. Also, unlike the treaty body mechanisms, it is not necessary to have exhausted all domestic remedies before submitting a complaint and indeed, the complaint may be lodged with both a treaty body and a special procedure. A limitation is that special procedures are not legally binding mechanisms and so it is at each State's discretion to comply with the recommendations.[74] Nonetheless, we know that treaty body views are not in fact legally binding, even though the treaties themselves are and many States do not give effect to the recommendations made by treaty bodies in their 'views' on cases.

The communications of the Special Procedures is quite extensively used, generally achieves a positive outcome, but is not without risks. For example, from 2006 to 2018, the Special Rapporteur on the situation of human rights defenders received communications concerning more than 13,000 cases.[75] A survey of human rights defenders found that more than half of them were confident that the involvement of the Special Rapporteur had contributed to amelioration in their situation but a minority reported that

---

73 Nigel S Rodley, 'On the Responsibility of Special Rapporteurs' (2011) 15(2) *The International Journal of Human Rights* 319. See also United Nations High Commissioner for Human Rights, *Promotion and Protection of All Human Rights, Civil, Political, Economic, Social and Cultural Rights, Including the Right to Development*, 10th sess, Agenda Item 3, UN Doc A/HRC/10/24 (17 November 2008) paras 32–3; this had begun to operate *ad interim* in 2007.

74 *Civil Society Handbook*, UN Doc HR/PUB/06/10/Rev.1 (n 38) 158.

75 *Situation of Human Rights Defenders* UN Doc A/73/215 (n 68) 46.

communicating with the Special Rapporteur had contributed to a worsening of their situation.[76]

The second complaint mechanism then is that of the HRC, focusing on consistent patterns of gross violations of human rights, as opposed to individual cases. This procedure is also confidential, with a view to enhancing State cooperation. It was based on the Commission's 1503 procedure but with modifications to ensure that the procedure is impartial, objective, efficient, 'victims' oriented, and conducted in a timely manner.[77] The HRC Working Group on Situations is responsible for bringing consistent patterns of gross and reliably attested violations of human rights and fundamental freedoms to the attention of the HRC. The complaint procedure is universal – it covers all member States and all human rights – irrespective of treaty ratification.

6 The HRC advisory committee

The HRC is supported in its work by an Advisory Committee, with a strong emphasis on research and reflection. Paragraph 65 of the HRC Institution-building package provides for the HRC Advisory Committee, composed of 18 experts serving in their personal capacity, as a think-tank for the HRC.[78] The Advisory Committee cannot adopt resolutions or decisions, but can make suggestions to the HRC to enhance its procedural efficiency and to further research proposals within the scope of its work. The participation of NGOs in the work of the Advisory Committee is expressly supported in the Institution building package[79]:

> 82. In the performance of its mandate, the Advisory Committee is urged to establish interaction with States, national human rights institutions, non-governmental organizations, and other civil society entities in accordance with the modalities of the Council.
>
> 83. Member States and observers, including States that are not members of the Council, the specialized agencies, other intergovernmental organizations and national human rights institutions, as well as nongovernmental organizations shall be entitled to participate in the

---

76 Ibid.

77 United Nations Human Rights Council, 'Frequently Asked Questions' *Complaints Procedure* <www.ohchr.org/EN/HRBodies/HRC/ComplaintProcedure/Pages/FAQ.aspx>.

78 *Institution-Building of HRC*, UN Doc A/HRC/RES/5/1 (n 8) para 65.

79 Ibid para 3(m).

work of the Advisory Committee based on arrangements, including Economic and Social Council resolution 1996/31.

Some NGO representatives report that they felt heard by the Advisory Committee, that the role of NGOs is acknowledged by the Committee, and that civil society participation is encouraged.[80]

7 HRC subsidiary bodies and other opportunities for NGOs

There are a number of other relevant groups and fora of relevance to NGOs and which ones are most useful depends on the human rights focus area of the NGO. Key fora not already discussed earlier include the Expert Mechanism on the Rights of Indigenous People ('EMRIP'), the Forum on Minority Issues, the Social Forum, the Forum on Business and Human Rights, and the Forum on Human Rights, Democracy and the Rule of Law.

EMRIP is worth particular mention given its significance for Indigenous rights at the UN. It was part of the new architecture of the HRC and was established in 2007 by HRC Resolution 6/36,[81] to continue some of the work of the UN Working Group on Indigenous Populations ('WGIP') established by ECOSOC in 1982.[82] Its mandate was amended in September 2016 by HRC Resolution 33/25,[83] and it is now responsible for providing the HRC with expertise and advice on the rights of Indigenous peoples in the United Nations Declaration on the Rights of Indigenous Peoples ('UNDRIP') and support Member States to achieve the ends of the UNDRIP. Indigenous peoples are supported to participate in EMRIP – and other UN human rights bodies – through the UN Voluntary Fund for Indigenous Peoples.[84]

80 United Nations Human Rights Council, *Advisory Committee* <www.ohchr.org/EN/HRbodies/HRC/advisorycommittee/Pages/HRCACIndex.aspx>.

81 Human Rights Council, *Expert Mechanism on the Rights of Indigenous People*, 6th sess, 34th mtg, UN Doc A/HRC/RES/6/36 (14 December 2007).

82 To read an in-depth analysis of Indigenous peoples and the UN, see Rhiannon Morgan, *Transforming Law and Institution: Indigenous Peoples, the United Nations and Human Rights* (Routledge, 2011).

83 Human Rights Council, *Expert Mechanism on the Rights of Indigenous Peoples*, 33rd sess, 41st mtg, Agenda Item 5, UN Doc A/HRC/RES/33/25 (5 October 2016).

84 General Assembly, *Indigenous Issues*, UN GAOR, 3rd Comm, 63rd sess, 70th plen mtg, Agenda Item 61, A/RES/63/161 (13 February 2009). To read more about the UN Voluntary Fund for Indigenous Peoples, see Office of the High Commissioner for Human Rights, *UN Voluntary Fund for Indigenous People* <www.ohchr.org/EN/Issues/IPeoples/IPeoplesFund/Pages/IPeoplesFundIndex.aspx>.

The HRC also has a number of open-ended intergovernmental working groups that may be of interest to NGOs, again, depending on each NGO's area of interest. The working groups are generally charged with developing new draft legal instruments or making recommendations on existing instruments. These include: the Working Group on the Right to Development, the Intergovernmental Working Group on the Durban Declaration and Programme of Action, the Working Group on an Optional Protocol to the Convention on the Rights of the Child, the Open-ended intergovernmental working group on regulatory framework of activities of private military and security companies, the Open-ended intergovernmental working group on a draft United Nations declaration on the right to peace, and the Open-ended intergovernmental working group on transnational corporations and other business enterprises with respect to human rights.[85]

In Geneva, another useful way for NGOs (with ECOSOC accreditation) to engage relevant stakeholders is to organise a 'parallel event' on a topic of relevance to the HRC, or on the human rights situation of a State undergoing its UPR. These are often attended by State representatives, NHRIs, NGOs, Special Rapporteurs, and others. The use of parallel events by stakeholders requires further analysis though, following reports that resources companies from Western States were brought in to present at a parallel event to defend Eritrea's human rights record.[86]

8   Conclusion

One State representative I interviewed reflected: 'In Geneva, NGOs really have a huge role. The Human Rights Council is very open to NGOs, for example, NGOs can make statements and can participate in informal meetings regarding drafting of resolutions'.[87] Nonetheless, engagement with the HRC, and all UN human rights bodies, carries a risk for many NGOs and human rights defenders remain under threat around the world.

NGOs are recognised as a legitimate stakeholder at the HRC and play an important, albeit somewhat limited role. Governments are encouraged to consult with them in the UPR, other Governments display a willingness to hear their concerns, and there is some evidence that they influence the

---

85   To view the latest list of subsidiary bodies, visit Human Rights Council, *Human Rights Council Subsidiary Bodies* <www.ohchr.org/EN/HRBodies/HRC/Pages/OtherSubBodies.aspx>.

86   Human Rights Law Centre, 'Australian Mining Company Defends Eritrea at the UN' (14 March 2018) <www.hrlc.org.au/news/2018/3/13/australian-mining-company-defends-eritrea-at-the-un-2>.

87   McGaughey (n 7) 431.

recommendations made by States in the UPR. In addition to the UPR, there are a number of opportunities for NGO engagement and influence at the HRC, including the complaints procedures for a complaint on behalf of an individual to the relevant Special Rapporteur, or to report consistent patterns of gross and reliably attested violations of human rights. A wide range of opportunities also exist by engaging with the work of the thematic and country Special Procedures, the HRC's Advisory Committee, and other HRC subsidiary bodies.

6   Conclusion

1 Introduction

This book has charted the wide-ranging role and influence of NGOs in the UN human rights system. They are essential actors in the system, informing the development of international human rights law and supporting the monitoring of its implementation by providing critical information on the human rights situation on the ground. Despite pockets of reticence and occasional outright resistance and threats by States, the UN recognises and strongly values the NGO role. Wiseberg's 1991 assertion holds true. She posited that the UN human rights machinery 'would grind to a halt were it not fed by the fact-finding of human rights NGOs'.[1] Beyond contributing expertise in the drafting of international instruments, providing information and bringing complaints, NGOs also participate in global governance as part of a network of actors. Merry finds that NGOs can act as intermediaries so that international law can be adapted as a 'localized globalism',[2] resonating with Heyns and Vilijoen's conclusion that treaty norms must be internalised in the domestic legal and cultural system by harnessing 'domestic constituencies'.[3] Simply put, the UN human rights system needs NGOs.

2 Key themes

It is worth reflecting on a few overarching themes from the book in this final chapter. We have gained an insight into the work of NGOs and their nature. NGOs are tenacious and agile actors which have carefully and persistently

---

1 Laurie Wiseberg, 'Protecting Human Rights Activists and NGOs: What More Can Be Done?' (1991) 13(4) *Human Rights Quarterly* 525.

2 Merry, above n 77.

3 Christof Heyns and Frans Viljoen, *The Impact of the United Nations Human Rights Treaties on the Domestic Level* (Kluwer Law International, 2002) 6.

lobbied for a seat at the UN table. That they have succeeded in this quest is due to a number of factors, including their significant expertise in international human rights law and in its practical application on people around the globe. Nonetheless, it is important to remember that NGOs are not homogenous; Chapter 1 elucidates the complexity of defining NGOs and posits a taxonomy based on NGO functionality and their geographical reach. Future research could further develop the functional taxonomy of NGOs, to include other actors, such as NHRIs and other UN and international bodies. The increasing role of businesses due to the growing 'business and human rights' agenda also requires further research.

Although most often viewed as a post-World War II phenomenon, as discussed in Chapter 2, NGOs were active in the international arena for many years:

> Before the founding of the United Nations, NGOs led the charge in the adoption of some of the Declaration's forerunners. The Geneva conventions of 1864; multilateral labour conventions adopted in 1906; and the International Slavery Convention of 1926; all stemmed from the world of NGOs who infused the international community with a spirit of reform.[4]

They were active participants in the UN's predecessor, the League of Nations, and later, ensured that the UN Charter provided for human rights protection and promotion – and for a role for NGOs. This initial, limited consultative role under Article 71 of the Charter then gradually expanded over the years although not necessarily in a linear way as States often resisted NGO influence. By contributing expertise to the drafting of international instruments, including the Charter, the UDHR and human rights treaties, and by identifying opportunities created by the suite of UN human rights treaties, NGOs crafted a role for themselves, increasing in both numbers and influence.

The widening of NGO participation in UN human rights bodies over the decades now means there are a myriad of options for them. These are discussed in Chapters 4 and 5, together with the 'how to' of engagement and analysis of the potential for influence in each option. Key roles for NGOs include participation in treaty drafting and treaty interpretation through the development of general comments and general recommendations.

The State-reporting mechanisms of the HRC (through its UPR) and the treaty bodies, present significant, repeated, and ongoing opportunities for NGO input on States' ongoing compliance with UN treaties and international

---

4 Kofi Annan, 'Address to the 51st Annual DPI-NGO Conference' (Speech, United Nations, 1998).

human rights law more broadly. Engagement can take place via submission of reports, participating in informal briefings, or ideally, both. These cyclical mechanisms are significant, drawing on Koh's theory of transnational legal process, whereby various actors 'enforce' and internalise international law and through a 'repeated process of interaction and internalization' international law acquires its 'stickiness'.[5]

These bodies rely on information from NGOs on the actual human rights situation 'on the ground' when reviewing States' human rights performance. There are some differences in the two State-reporting mechanisms with regard to the scope for NGO influence – in summary the NGO role in the UPR is somewhat more limited than in treaty bodies. However, States appear to engage better with the UPR and there is more evidence on the rates of uptake and implementation of UPR recommendations, compared with those of treaty bodies. There is evidence of strong NGO influence on the recommendations developed by both sets of bodies – with some indications of stronger NGO influence on treaty body recommendations ('concluding observations') but overall there is more extensive empirical research available to date on influence in the UPR. The UPR and treaty body State-reporting mechanisms were intended to be complementary to each other as stated in Resolution 60/251,[6] and NGOs should view them as such. There are opportunities for NGO consultation with Government at a domestic level associated with the UN mechanisms; these can be used to reinforce key NGO messages and follow up on implementation of previous UN recommendations.

NGOs can also 'target' thematic and/or country Special Rapporteurs of relevance to their human rights agenda. Like treaty bodies, these independent experts are open to – and to some extent rely on – input from NGOs. Another area where NGOs are active is in bringing individual complaints, through either the relevant treaty body or the relevant Special Rapporteurs but they should consider the differences in these options as outlined in Chapter 5. The HRC also has a broader complaint mechanism to report consistent patterns of gross and reliably attested violations of human rights (rather than an individual complaint). Lastly, the HRC Advisory Committee and other HRC fora and working groups provide significant opportunities for NGO networking and influence, depending on their area of interest. Examples include: the Expert Mechanism on the Rights of Indigenous People

---

5 Harold Hongju Koh, 'Transnational Legal Process' (1996) 75 *Nebraska Law Review* 181, 198.
6 General Assembly Resolution 60/251, Human Rights Council, UN Doc A/RES/60/251, 3 April 2006.

('EMRIP') and the Forum on Business and Human Rights, and the Working Group on the Right to Development.[7]

In summary, there are many options but for NGOs which are often resource-poor, it is important to be strategic and consider the mechanism with which to engage. The mechanisms are also, to varying degrees, interconnected. For example, the UPR relies heavily on information from Special Rapporteurs and treaty bodies, so NGO influence can trickle through the system in this way.[8] The variety of opportunities for engagement with a range of actors, as well as the different nature of the UN bodies – the political HRC and the quasi-judicial treaty bodies – means that NGOs require an extensive repertoire of skills. Another strategic consideration for NGOs is the use of networks and coalitions. This theme emerged throughout the literature and in my interviews. Coalitions are seen as efficient and easier for experts, State representatives, and secretariats to engage with, but also as having more legitimacy and credibility due to the numbers of actors involved.

Chapter 4 discussed the drafting of the CRoC and the fact that the 'Informal NGO Ad Hoc Group on the Drafting of the Convention on the Rights of the Child' made a significant input to the text of the Convention. The literature, interview data, and some empirical evidence strongly emphasise the importance of working in coalitions for maximum influence on treaty body State reporting and the UPR. Both treaty bodies and the UPR encourage coalition reports. Nonetheless, forming a cohesive, coordinated NGO coalition, where diverse interests and issues are accommodated, can be challenging. This is even more pronounced in the UPR than in other mechanisms given the breadth of topics for consideration and the very tight word limit for reports. As outlined in the taxonomy in Chapter 1, the relationship between domestic and international NGOs can be both beneficial and challenging. In some cases, domestic NGOs may be more influential. Simmons and Merry proposed that whilst transnational networks may be critical in the case of a repressive regime, in most States domestic actors are the most significant.[9]

---

7 To view the latest list of subsidiary bodies, visit Human Rights Council, *Human Rights Council Subsidiary Bodies* <www.ohchr.org/EN/HRBodies/HRC/Pages/OtherSubBodies. aspx>.

8 For examples and further analysis see Fiona McGaughey, 'The Role and Influence of Non-Governmental Organisations in the Universal Periodic Review – International Context and Australian Case Study' (2017) 17(3) *Human Rights Law Review* 421.

9 Sally Engle Merry, *Human Rights and Gender Violence: Translating International Law into Local Justice* (University of Chicago Press, 2006); Beth Simmons, *Mobilizing for Human Rights: International Law in Domestic Politics* (Cambridge University Press, 2009).

All stakeholders have concerns with the current regime of NGO regulation in UN human rights bodies. Apart from obvious challenges, such as funding and resources, NGO engagement at the UN is fettered in a number of ways as discussed in Chapter 3. At worst, human rights defenders are threatened or 'disappeared' and some States will consistently contest the NGO role. Most States accept or even welcome the NGO role but support regulation that restricts some access. For maximum participation at the HRC, ECOSOC accreditation is required,[10] and the associated decision-making process by the Committee on NGOs has been extensively criticised for its lack of transparency and alleged politicisation. Many of the 'day-to-day' opportunities for influential NGO engagement with UN human rights bodies do not require accreditation. This opens access more broadly to a range of NGOs, but can also cause problems for those in UN bodies receiving an influx of information, sometimes from questionable sources, such as GONGOs. Through a regulatory pluralism lens, we can see other forms of regulation at play, including filtering out of NGO information and gatekeeping of UN bodies. Future research could support the UN to strike a reasonable balance between ascertaining the legitimacy of NGOs and managing their engagement with UN bodies from a logistical perspective, while not unduly limiting NGO access.

3 Parting words

To conclude, the monitoring of international human rights law must be done from both above and below. NGOs play an essential role, as do States, UN experts, NHRIs, and other actors. The evidence in this book is clear that NGOs play a significant role. They are a critical component of the international human rights legal machinery and their voices, and the voices of those they represent must continue to be heard:

> Metaphorically, voice constitutes a social geography mapped and measured by the distance needed to create a sense of engagement. More literally, voice is about meaningful conversation and power. . . . Power suggests that the conversation makes a difference: Our voices are heard and have some impact on the direction of the process and the decisions made.[11]

---

10 *Consultative Relationship between the United Nations and Non-Governmental Organizations,* ECOSOC Res1996/31, 49th plen mtg, UN Doc E/RES/1996/31 (25 July 1996).
11 John Paul Lederach, *The Moral Imagination: The Art and Soul of Building Peace* (Oxford University Press, 2005) 56.

At the time of writing, the COVID-19 pandemic continues to sweep the globe. This has provided challenges for many sectors, including the NGO sector. Those organisations which also provide services and humanitarian assistance have been inundated in many countries and for those with an advocacy function, the significant and widespread restrictions imposed by Governments warrants keen scrutiny and oversight from above (UN human rights bodies) and below (NGOs). Concomitantly, the pandemic and associated travel limitations and social distancing requirements have led to new modus operandi for many, moving meetings 'online' and opening up new channels of communication. This could present an opportunity to develop better online engagement between NGOs and the UN, although the 'digital divide' exists and access to technology, reliable internet, and unfettered online freedom remain challenges in many countries and regions.[12] Although there were some pockets of good practice in this regard, such as some treaty bodies engaging with NGO delegations via video conferencing, this was by no means common practice. Given the significant resources required to participate at UN fora in Geneva and the particular challenges this poses for NGOs from the Global South and for a sector that typically struggles for funding, more online participation could revolutionise NGO engagement at the UN.

NGOs have demonstrated their tenacity and flexibility for many decades and no doubt will continue to do so despite mounting global challenges, such as pandemics and climate change. They are an essential cog in the machinery of the UN human rights system and as such, may have exceeded the expectations of Eleanor Roosevelt who predicted they would play an indispensable role as the 'curious grapevine' that would enlighten people about their rights and channel information about human rights violations to the world.[13]

---

12 Office of the High Commissioner for Human Rights, *Human Rights Council Holds Panel Discussion on Emerging Digital Technologies; Begins Interactive Dialogue with Special Rapporteur on Internally Displaced Persons* (8 July 2020). <www.ohchr.org/EN/NewsEvents/Pages/DisplayNews.aspx?NewsID=26054&LangID=E>.

13 William Korey, 'Human Rights NGOS: The Power of Persuasion' (1999) 13(1) *Ethics & International Affairs* 151.

Index

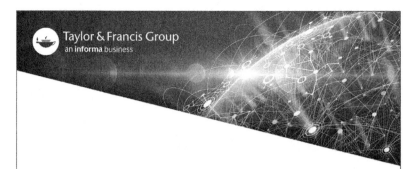

Printed in the United States
by Baker & Taylor Publisher Services